Country Interiors
Intérieurs à la campagne

Diane Dorrans Saeks

Country Interiors
Intérieurs à la campagne

Edited by | Sous la direction de | Herausgegeben von

Angelika Taschen

TASCHEN

KÖLN LONDON MADRID NEW YORK PARIS TOKYO

Endpapers | Pages de garde | Vorsatzpapier:
Romantic landscape in Périgord
Paysage romantique du Périgord
Romantische Landschaft im Périgord
Photo: Andreas von Einsiedel
(pages 84–95)

Page 2: The porch of Berns Fry and Ricks Lee on Long Island
Page 2: Le porche chez Berns Fry et Ricks Lee sur Long Island
Seite 2: Die Veranda von Berns Fry und Ricks Lee auf Long Island
Photo: Pieter Estersohn
(pages 246–253)

Page 7: A young deer near the chalet of Richard Stadler in Tyrol
Page 7: Un jeune chevreuil près du chalet de Richard Stadler dans le Tyrol
Seite 7: Ein junges Reh bei dem Chalet von Richard Stadler in Tirol
Photo: Eric Laignel & Patricia Parinejad
(pages 114–117)

Texts edited by Ursula Fethke, Cologne; Petra Frese, Dortmund
Production by Horst Neuzner, Cologne
French translation by Philippe Safavi, Paris
German translation by Kornelia Stuckenberger, Munich,
and Clara Drechsler, Cologne (preface)

Printed in Spain

ISBN 3–8228–5886–2

Contents
Sommaire
Inhalt

Green Worlds
By Diane Dorrans Saeks

Des mondes de verdure
Par Diane Dorrans Saeks

Grüne Welten
Von Diane Dorrans Saeks

Life is sweet. Spring green poplars rustle in the early morning breeze as a man in a jaunty straw hat and a pair of old, ripped jeans walks silently in his rose garden. Away across the dew-drenched meadow the mist is clearing and this promises to be the perfect country day of gathering weeds, watching leafy green branches swing through the air, and wandering down to a light-stippled stream to pick watercress for a luncheon salad under the trees. Immersed in his green world, the man clips his beloved *New Dawn* and *Maréchal Niel* roses. For the moment, only the caress of the warm sun on the nape of his neck, the mysteries hidden in each naked tendril of honeysuckle, and the simple glory of each moment exist.

Further north on the island of Gotland in the Baltic, a young family watches clouds chase across the pearlescent autumn sky. For hours they walk through the fields sensing the flight of birds. They listen to dry grasses crackling beneath their feet, and smell oak leaves, sweet berries, the earthy scent of mushrooms and moss-tangled ferns.

The countryside does not demand that we fill our days and our minds with ambitious plans. We can depart from the created world, and slip into an edenic grace. In the warm green heart of Ibiza, a lazy afternoon on the terrace is scented with the sharp fragrances of pine and lavender. And along the rock-strewn cliffs of the Hudson River in New York, a house hides among the trees, and nature seems to have gained the upper hand.

In the country, self-expression is in the air. In France, an improbably large gold bed stands in the glory of an old farmhouse, like a guest wearing a glittering couture ballgown at a country fair.

A Dutch artist feathers her nest with bowers of goosedown and a baldacchino crowned with feathers and lavish jewels.

Life in the country is waiting to be created. Shakespeare evokes the magical power of nature in "As You Like It". In Act Two, Scene One, set in the Forest of Arden, the Senior Duke intones:
"And this our life, exempt from public haunt,
Finds tongues in trees, books in the running brooks,
Sermons in stones, and good in every thing."

Ce que la vie est douce... La brise du petit matin fait frémir les peupliers vert printemps tandis qu'un homme portant un fringant chapeau de paille et une vieille paire de jeans déchirés arpente en silence sa roseraie. De l'autre côté du pré détrempé par la rosée, la brume matinale se dissipe et laisse entrevoir les prémisses d'une journée parfaite pour arracher les mauvaises herbes, contempler le balancement des branches feuillues ou patauger dans un ruisseau pour cueillir du cresson. Plongé dans son monde de verdure, l'homme taille ses chères roses *New Dawn* et *Maréchal Niel*. Pour le moment, seuls existent la caresse chaude du soleil sur sa nuque, les mystères cachés sous les vrilles nues du chèvrefeuille et la beauté simple de l'instant qui passe.

Plus au nord, sur l'île de Gotland, dans la mer Baltique, une jeune famille scrute les nuages. Pendant des heures, ils écoutent les herbes sèches craquer sous leurs pas et hument l'odeur des feuilles mortes, des baies sucrées, les effluves des champignons et des fougères prises dans la mousse. Au cœur de l'île verte et ensoleillée d'Ibiza, le parfum enivrant des pins et de la lavande parfume les après-midi paresseux sur la terrasse. Parmi les rochers éboulés au pied des falaises qui bordent l'Hudson dans l'Etat de New York, une maison se cache entre les arbres et semble sur le point d'être engloutie par la végétation.

La campagne invite à l'expression personnelle. En France, un grand lit doré se dresse incongrûment dans la beauté dépouillée d'une vieille ferme, tel une invitée en robe du soir haute couture débarquant dans une guinguette. Une artiste hollandaise garnit son nid de duvet d'oie et crée des baldaquins couronnés de bijoux et de plumes.

La vie à la campagne attend d'être créée. Dans «Comme il vous plaira», dont l'action se situe dans la forêt des Ardennes, Shakespeare évoque le pouvoir magique de la nature. Acte II, scène un, le Vieux Duc déclame:

«Cette existence à l'abri de la cohue publique
révèle des voix dans les arbres,
des livres dans les ruisseaux qui coulent,
des leçons dans les pierres
et le bien en toute chose.»

Das Leben ist süß. Frühlingsgrüne Pappeln rascheln im leisen Wind des frühen Morgens und ein Mann in verschlissenen Jeans, einen alten Strohhut auf dem Kopf, geht schweigend durch seinen Rosengarten. Weiter hinten über den taufeuchten Wiesen hebt sich der Dunst und verspricht einen perfekten Tag auf dem Land, der dazu einlädt, Unkraut zu jäten, zu beobachten, wie belaubte Zweige hin und her schwingen oder zu einem mit Lichttupfen gesprenkelten Bachlauf hinunterzubummeln und dort Brunnenkresse zu zupfen für einen Salat zum Mittagessen unter den Bäumen. In diese grüne Welt versunken, stutzt der Mann seine geliebten *New Dawn* und *Maréchal Niel*-Rosen und für den Moment existieren nur die sanfte Berührung des Sonnenlichts in seinem Nacken, die Geheimnisse, die in jeder Geißblattranke schlummern, und die schlichte Herrlichkeit jedes einzelnen Moments.

Auf Gotland schaut eine junge Familie den Wolken nach, die der Herbstwind über den perlmuttglänzenden Himmel jagt. Sie wandern für Stunden über die Felder, wo sie den Flügelschlag der Vögel spüren. Das Land entlässt uns aus der Pflicht, unsere Tage mit ehrgeizigen Plänen auszufüllen, sondern wir dürfen in paradiesische Anmut eintauchen. Im warmen, grünen Herzen Ibizas liegt über einem schläfrigen Nachmittag auf der Terrasse der aromatische Duft von Pinien und Lavendel. Entlang der felsigen Uferklippen des Hudson River im Bundesstaat New York versteckt sich ein Haus in den Bäumen und es scheint, als hätte die Natur die Oberhand gewonnen.

Die Landluft animiert zur Selbstentfaltung. In Frankreich steht ein großes, goldenes Bett in einem alten Bauernhaus wie eine große Dame, die in einem glitzernden Ballkleid zu einer Dorfkirmes erschienen ist. Eine holländische Künstlerin versieht ihr Nest mit Gänsedaunen sowie einem mit Federn und Edelsteinen geschmückten Baldachin.

Leben auf dem Lande heißt noch darauf warten, erschaffen zu werden. Shakespeare schildert diesen Zauber der Natur in »Wie es euch gefällt«. Im 2. Akt, 1. Szene, sagt der alte Herzog im Ardenner Wald:

»Dies unser Leben, vom Getümmel frei,
Gibt Bäumen Zungen, findet Schrift im Bach,
In Steinen Lehre, Gutes überall.«

Groddagården

Fleringe, Gotland, Sweden

*Dans le nord de l'île de Gotland, on est particulièrement fier de Grod-
dagården, une ferme-auberge en pierre du 17e siècle et devenue aujourd'hui un musée d'histoire folklorique. Autour de 1700, la famille
Grodde s'installa dans cette bâtisse fortifiée comptant trois chambres
à coucher. A partir de 1781, Groddagården fut surnommée «la maison
des violonistes» en raison des violonistes et gambistes qui venaient y
jouer pour les propriétaires des lieux. Les intérieurs étaient alors lam-
brissés de planches de sapin, avec de petites portes et des murs plâtrés
blanchis à la chaux, typiques de ces petits espaces intimes. Les
meubles en sapin étaient simples et sans prétention. En 1850, de nouveaux propriétaires plus prospères introduisirent une touche de fantai-
sie et ornèrent les murs de la salle à manger d'une frise au pochoir gar-
nie de lyres, de guirlandes et de fleurs. La cheminée en plâtre se donna
de grands airs avec un trompe-l'œil de marbre peint dans le plus pur
style folklorique. De talentueux artistes voyageaient dans toute la
Scandinavie pour réaliser ces charmantes décorations.*

In northern Gotland, islanders are especially proud of Groddagården, a 17th-century stone farmhouse and hostelry which has become a folkloric history museum. Since around 1700, the Grodde
family dwelt in the shelter of this fortress-like, three-bedroom
stone house. Groddagården became known as the Fiddlers'
House after 1781, for the skilled fiddlers and crank-lyre players who
gathered to perform with the family. The interiors display pine
panelling walls, small doorways, whitewashed plaster walls typical
of these intimate spaces. Pine furniture was simple and unpreten-
tious. In contrast, in 1850 the prosperous owners introduced a
touch of fantasy, and stencilled the walls in the dining room with a
flourish of lyres, garlands and flowers. The plaster fireplace puts
on grand airs with a bravura display of faux marbre painting in the
best folkloric style. Skilled artists traveled throughout Scandinavia
producing these charming and enduring decorations.

*Die Gotländer im Norden der Insel sind besonders stolz auf Grod-
dagården, ein Bauern- und Wirtshaus aus dem 17. Jahrhundert, das
heute ein Heimatmuseum ist. In dem festungsartigen Haus, das in
Steinbauweise errichtet wurde und über drei Schlafzimmer verfügt,
lebte ab etwa 1700 die Familie Grodde. Nach 1781 wurde Groddagården auch »Haus der Geigenspieler« genannt, weil dort oft Geiger und
Drehorgelspieler für die Familie musizierten. Die Innenräume sind
zum Teil mit Kiefernholz verschalt, es gibt kleine Türeingänge und
weiß getünchte Wände, wie sie typisch für diese Gegend sind. Die Möbel aus Kiefernholz waren schlicht und unprätentiös. Nach 1850
wechselte das Haus die Besitzer, die neuen Eigentümer waren wohl-
habend und ließen mehr Fantasie walten. Die Wände im Esszimmer
bekamen Verzierungen aus Girlanden, Lyren und Blumenmustern,
die mit Hilfe von Schablonen aufgetragen wurden. Die eindrucksvol-
len Kamineinfassungen prunkten mit imitiertem Marmor, den rei-
sende Handwerker in bestem rustikalem Stil auf Gips aufmalten.*

Facing page and above: Fireplaces retained heat to warm these rooms, and the heavy-set plaster surround retained heat to cozy each room. Windows were small and thick plaster walls created ultra-deep reveals. The farmer-owners of the house painted a low contrasting wainscot to give the effect of more complex detailing. Today the air here smells of pine, fish and smoke, and voices of the farm families and fiddlers, and bellowing cows seem to waft in from the green meadows beyond the walls.

Page de gauche et ci-dessus: Pour chauffer ces pièces, les cheminées étaient indispensables. Leur épais manteau de plâtre retenait la chaleur. Les fenêtres étaient petites et les murs formaient des embrasures très profondes. Les agriculteurs qui possédaient cette maison ont peint le lambris bas d'une couleur contrastante pour donner un effet de profondeur. Aujourd'hui, l'air sent le sapin, le poisson et la fumée. Les voix des familles de la ferme et des violonistes se joignent aux meuglements des vaches et semblent flotter depuis les prés de l'autre côté des murs.

Linke Seite und oben: Geheizt wurde mit offenen Kaminen und der rundum dick aufgetragene Putz half, die Wärme zu speichern. Die Fenster sind schmal und besonders tief in die dick verputzten Mauern eingeschnitten. Die in gedeckten Farben aufgemalte Vertäfelung gibt den Räumen Struktur. Heute riecht es hier nach Kiefern, Fisch und Rauch und man glaubt, die Stimmen der Bauernfamilie und der Geigenspieler und das Muhen der Kühe auf den sattgrünen Wiesen durch die Mauern zu hören.

Tor Halvorsen

Eina, Oppland, Norway

*Amis depuis plus de 20 ans, Tor Halvorsen et Benthe Stiansen ont tou-
jours eu la joyeuse habitude d'échanger leurs maisons. Lorsque Benthe
et sa famille ont acheté cette ferme du siècle dernier près d'Eina, un
village à 110 kilomètres au nord d'Oslo, il était donc tout naturel que
Tor s'y installe aussi. Artiste touche-à-tout, décorateur, visagiste, styliste de photo et poète basé dans la capitale norvégienne, il a établi sa
retraite de week-end dans la vieille grange où hivernaient autrefois les
chevaux et les vaches. «Au fond, je suis un vrai garçon de ferme», plai-
sante-t-il. Dans la carcasse en rondins de bois de la grange, il s'est
construit un loft sur deux niveaux, incluant une cuisine moderne «à
l'ancienne» et un atelier à la lumière somptueuse. «Toute maison est
un portrait de celui qui l'habite», reconnaît-il. Les nuits d'été, Tor re-
joint Benthe Stiansen sur la terrasse de cette dernière qui domine un
lac et tous deux discutent poésie, existence et philosophie sous un ciel
scintillant d'étoiles.*

Tor Halvorsen and Benthe Stiansen have been friends for more
than 20 years, and during this time have had the happy habit of
swapping houses. When Benthe and her family acquired a century-old farm near the village of Eina, 70 miles north of Oslo, it
was only natural that Tor would spend time there. He decided to
make a weekend retreat in the century-old timber barn where
horses and cows had sheltered in the winter. "I'm really a farm
boy," joked Halvorsen, a polymath artist, interior designer, hair
stylist, photo stylist and poet who lives in Oslo. Working within
the log skeleton of the muscular old barn, Halvorsen built a two-
level loft, complete with a kitchen, and a superbly lit painting studio. "Every home is a portrait of the owner's personality," admit-
ted Halvorsen, who on summer nights joins Stiansen on her
terrace overlooking a lake, to discuss poetry, life, and philosophy
as stars sparkle like diamonds overhead.

*Tor Halvorsen und Benthe Stiansen sind seit über 20 Jahren befreun-
det und während all dieser Zeit hatten sie die schöne Angewohnheit,
ihre Wohnungen zu tauschen. Als Benthe und ihre Familie einen 100
Jahre alten Bauernhof in der Nähe der Kleinstadt Eina erwarben, 110
Kilometer nördlich von Oslo, war es ganz normal, dass Tor dort einige
Zeit verbrachte. Er beschloss, in einer dazugehörigen alten Holz-
scheune, in der früher Pferde und Kühe im Winter untergebracht waren, sein Wochenendhaus einzurichten. »Ich bin nämlich ein Junge
vom Land«, scherzt Halvorsen, ein vielseitiger Künstler, Interior-
Designer, Hairstylist, Fotostylist und Lyriker, der in Oslo lebt. Halvorsen ließ die Holzträger der mächtigen alten Scheune stehen und
baute ein Loft über zwei Ebenen mit einer Küche und einem licht-
durchfluteten Atelier. »Jede Wohnung spiegelt die Persönlichkeit des
Eigentümers wider«, meint Halvorsen. In den Sommernächten sitzt
er mit Benthe Stiansen auf ihrer Terrasse mit Blick auf den See, und
während sie über Poesie, Philosophie und das Leben an sich diskutie-
ren, funkeln über ihren Köpfen diamantene Sterne.*

Previous pages: In winter, Halvorsen uses a "spark" (the traditional Norwegian snow sled) to go to the village. The old barn door is decorated with ceramic fish. For his bedroom, Halvorsen used vintage Swedish linen bed sheets. Placed above the bed is an eight-faceted dome he painted to look like an old fresco.
Above and right: the living room. In a corner Tor placed a plaster Aphrodite.

Double page précédente: L'hiver, Halvorsen se rend au village en «spark», le traîneau traditionnel norvégien. La porte de la vieille grange est ornée d'un poisson en céramique. Dans sa chambre, il dort dans des draps anciens en lin suédois. Il a peint le dôme octogonal au-dessus de son lit à la manière d'une fresque ancienne.
Ci-dessus et à droite: le salon. Dans un coin, Tor a placé une Aphrodite en plâtre.

Vorhergehende Doppelseite: Im Winter fährt Halvorsen mit einem »spark«, dem traditionellen norwegischen Schlitten, ins Dorf. Keramikfische zieren das alte Scheunentor. In seinem Schlafzimmer verwendet er alte schwedische Leinenbettwäsche. Über dem Bett wölbt sich eine achtseitige Kuppel, die Tor im Stil alter Fresken bemalte.
Oben und rechts: das Wohnzimmer. In einer Ecke steht eine Aphroditestatue aus Gips.

Eina, Oppland, Norway   Tor Halvorsen

Tor, who has exhibited his paintings in Oslo galleries, built himself a painting studio. Norwegians traditionally built crosses on doors and windows to prevent witches from stealing the farm animals or food.

Halvorsen, qui expose ses tableaux dans des galeries d'Oslo, s'est construit un atelier. Depuis toujours, les Norvégiens posent des croix sur leurs portes et leurs fenêtres pour empêcher les sorcières de leur voler leurs bêtes ou leur nourriture.

Halvorsen, der in Galerien in Oslo ausstellt, baute für sich ein Atelier. Die Holzkreuze auf Türen und Fenstern sollen nach einer traditionellen norwegischen Vorstellung Hexen daran hindern, Tiere oder Vorräte zu stehlen.

Eina, Oppland, Norway

Tor Halvorsen

The kitchen floor and walls were painted with five different white hues to tone them down.

Le sol et les murs de la cuisine ont été peints de cinq tons de blanc différents jusqu'à atteindre une douce patine.

Fußboden und Wände in der Küche wurden in fünf verschiedenen Weißtönen aufeinander abgestimmt.

Tor has been decorating his rooms since he was 12 years old. He juxtaposes a French Art Nouveau candelabra with a tramp art mirror and a hand-hewn log wall. In true rustic chic style, an old knit sweater is turned into a pillow, a trio of Gustavian chairs is gilded and painted, and a silver punch bowl serves chanterelle soup.

Tor décore ses pièces depuis qu'il a douze ans. Ici, il a juxtaposé un chandelier français Art nouveau avec un miroir de récupération et un mur en planches de bois brut. Dans un vrai style «chic rustique», un vieux pull en laine a été transformé en coussin et un trio de chaises gustaviennes ont été peintes et dorées. Une soupe aux chanterelles fume dans une coupe à punch en argent.

Bereits mit 12 Jahren begann Tor damit, sein Zimmer selbst zu dekorieren. Vor der groben Holzwand steht ein französischer Art-Nouveau-Kerzenleuchter neben einem originell verzierten Spiegel. Perfektes Country-Ambiente: ein Strickpullover verwandelte sich in ein Kissen, drei Stühle im gustavianischen Stil wurden vergoldet und bemalt und aus dem silbernen Bowlengefäß wird Pfifferlingsuppe serviert.

Eina, Oppland, Norway

Tor Halvorsen

Halvorsen's restless creativity has led him to master many decorative techniques. He can gild mirrors, create pebble patterns in the concrete floor of his bathroom, and paint turquoise and rust faux "water marks" on the barn's white board and batten walls. His motto, written on the kitchen wall, "Life is not easy, only fantastic."

Infatigable créatif, Tor a appris à maîtriser de nombreuses techniques décoratives. Il sait dorer les miroirs, a réalisé la mosaïque de galets dans le sol en ciment de sa salle de bains, a peint le trompe-l'œil de «taches d'humidité» turquoise et rouille sur les planches en bois blancs de sa grange. Sa devise, écrite sur le mur de la cuisine est: «La vie est dure, mais fantastique.»

Neugier und Kreativität führten dazu, dass Halvorsen heute viele Dekorationstechniken beherrscht. Er vergoldet Spiegel, legt auf dem Betonfußboden im Badezimmer Mosaike aus Kieselsteinen und malt türkis- und rostfarbene falsche »Wasserspuren« auf die weiße Holztäfelung. Sein Motto steht auf der Küchenwand: »Das Leben ist nicht leicht, nur fantastisch.«

The simple white wood bathroom. Halvorsen's friends from Oslo love to drive up and visit him in his bucolic setting. On long summer days, they venture out to Lake Mjøsa, Norway's largest lake.

La sobre salle de bains en bois blanc. Ses amis d'Oslo adorent rendre visite à Halvorsen dans ce décor bucolique. Pendant les longs jours d'été, ils s'aventurent jusqu'au lac Mjøsa, le plus grand de Norvège.

Das schlichte, mit weiß gestrichenem Holz vertäfelte Badezimmer. Die Freunde kommen gerne aus Oslo herauf, um Tor in seiner ländlichen Idylle zu besuchen. An langen Sommertagen fahren sie zum Mjøsa-See hinaus, dem größten See Norwegens.

Eina, Oppland, Norway

Tor Halvorsen

At the end of a long country day, guests retire to a capacious sleeping loft, complete with a grand bed with a thick velour coverlet.

Après une journée bien remplie, les invités se retirent dans le spacieux grenier-chambre à coucher, où les attend une couche somptueuse drapée d'un moelleux couvre-lit en velours.

Am Ende eines langen Tages auf dem Land ziehen sich die Gäste in das geräumige Schlafzimmer zurück, in dem ein großes Bett mit einer dicken Tagesdecke aus Samt steht.

Celia Lyttelton

Yorkshire, Great Britain

L'artiste Celia Lyttelton se souvient encore de la première fois où elle est tombée sur son cottage de tisserands du 17e siècle, «Overwood», au détour d'une promenade avec son père dans ce coin reculé du Yorkshire. Modestement bâtie dans une vallée boisée, la bâtisse surplombe un petit torrent et se trouve à proximité à pied de Top Withins, la lande balayée par les vents qui a inspiré le site naturel théâtral des «Hauts de Hurlevent». Tombée amoureuse de ce site sauvage, Lyttelton décida de la louer. Il a fallu plusieurs années pour nettoyer les gravats. Le matériel de construction fut acheminé en brouette par un sentier tortueux. Avec l'aide de ses amis maçons, Bill Beeton et Raven Dominic, Celia Lyttelton a reconstruit les cheminées, enduit les murs de plâtre et transformé la grange en atelier de gravure. Amis et parents ont apporté leur contribution sous forme de tissus anciens de Bennison et d'un kilim anatolien élimé «juste ce qu'il faut». Des amis artistes ont offert des tableaux colorés. Dans cette région encore hantée par Daniel Defoe et les sœurs Brontë, la créativité reste de mise.

Artist Celia Lyttelton recalls that she first came upon her 17th-century weavers' cottage, "Overwood", while out walking in a remote corner of Yorkshire with her father. Built modestly in a wooded valley, the house overlooked a rushing river and was within hiking distance of Top Withins, the windswept moor that inspired the dramatic location of "Wuthering Heights". Lyttelton was captivated by the wild and poetic setting, and arranged a lease. For several years she cleared debris. Building materials were brought down a rough path by wheelbarrow. Lyttelton and friends, builders Bill Beeton and Raven Dominic, rebuilt fireplaces, plastered walls, and turned the barn into an etching studio. Friends and family assisted with vintage Bennison fabrics and a deliciously worn Anatolian Kilim, and artist chums offered up colorful paintings. In a region where authors like Daniel Defoe and the Brontë sisters all rambled, creativity was nourished.

Die Künstlerin Celia Lyttelton erinnert sich gerne daran, wie sie bei einem Spaziergang mit ihrem Vater zum ersten Mal »Overwood« sah, ein ehemaliges Weber-Cottage aus dem 17. Jahrhundert. Versteckt in einem bewaldeten Tal blickt es auf einen reißenden Fluss und nur einen Fußmarsch entfernt liegt Top Withins, ein windgepeitschtes Moor, das den dramatischen Hintergrund für den Roman »Sturmhöhe« lieferte. Celia Lyttelton war gefangen von dieser wild-poetischen Landschaft und beschloss, das Haus zu mieten. Mehrere Jahre lang räumte sie erst einmal Schutt weg. Die Baumaterialien mussten mit einem Schubkarren über einen holprigen Weg hergebracht werden. Lyttelton und ihre Freunde Bill Beeton und Raven Dominic, beide im Baugewerbe tätig, setzten neue Kamine, verputzten Wände und machten aus der alten Scheune ein Studio, in dem Celia heute an ihren Radierungen arbeitet. Freunde und Familie schenkten ihr alte Bennison-Stoffe und einen herrlichen alten anatolischen Kelim und von Künstlerkollegen erhielt sie Gemälde in ausdrucksvollen Farben. Hier, im Land von Daniel Defoe und den Brontë-Schwestern, kann sich Kreativität frei entfalten.

Previous pages: *The former weavers' house was blessed with tall windows which drew light into the plaster-walled rooms.*
Above and right: *A capacious antique daybed, discovered in the region, serves as a boat to carry readers and dreamers alike off to a distant land. Lyttelton's fine sense of color and texture is evident in the rich hues she mixed for the walls. Raw pigments in odd, warm tones were mixed into the plaster and thinned to the perfect consistency with rabbit skin glue. Celia persisted in working on the fireplace and chimney, against all odds, and finally made it work.*

Double page précédente: *Cette ancienne maison de tisserands possède de hautes fenêtres qui illuminent les murs enduits de plâtre.*
Ci-dessus et à droite: *Dans le spacieux lit de repos ancien, découvert dans la région, les lecteurs et les rêveurs embarquent pour des contrées imaginaires et lointaines. Lyttelton a un sens aigu des couleurs et des matières, comme en attestent les tons riches qu'elle a choisis pour ses murs. Des pigments bruts aux teintes chaudes et inhabituelles ont été mélangés au plâtre puis dilués avec de la colle de peau de lapin jusqu'à obtenir la consistance parfaite. Persévérante, Lyttelton s'est échinée à restaurer les cheminées et leurs conduits jusqu'à ce qu'elles se remettent à marcher.*

Vorhergehende Doppelseite: *Das ehemalige Weber-Haus hat hohe Fenster, durch die das Licht auf die verputzten Wände fällt.*
Oben und rechts: *Ein tiefes, antikes Tagesbett, das Celia in der Nähe entdeckte, lädt zu einer Fantasiereise in ein fernes Land ein. Lytteltons ausgeprägter Sinn für Farben und Texturen zeigt sich an den feinabgestuften Farbschattierungen der Wände, die sie selbst mischte. Grobe Pigmente in gebrochenen, warmen Farben wurden mit dem Putz vermischt und mit Hasenleim verdünnt, bis die richtige Konsistenz erreicht war.*

Yorkshire, Great Britain   Celia Lyttelton

Right: Windows overlooked a small garden, and views of moorland and ancient oaks. It's little wonder friends and artists came to visit or work in Celia Lyttelton's etching studio – and stayed for weeks or months. Certainly the location is remote, and winters can be snowy, but it is the easy-going style of the house that made it impossible to leave.

Below: Celia became a happy scavenger, merrily and arduously restoring and cleaning a large trestle table and beechwood dining chairs which she discovered among the debris of the deserted house.

A droite: Les fenêtres donnent sur un petit jardin, des fragments de landes et des chênes séculaires. Il n'y a rien d'étonnant à ce que des amis et artistes venus en visite ou pour travailler dans l'atelier de Celia soient restés des semaines et des mois. Certes, le coin est isolé et les hivers sont enneigés, mais c'est surtout l'art de vivre nonchalant qui règne dans la maison qui les a retenus.

Ci-dessous: Celia est passée maître dans l'art de la récupération, restaurant joyeusement et laborieusement cette grande table montée sur tréteaux et ces chaises en hêtre retrouvées dans les débris de la bâtisse abandonnée.

Rechts: Aus den Fenstern blickt man in einen kleinen Garten und auf das dahinterliegende Moor und alte Eichen. Freunde auf Besuch oder Künstler, die in Celia Lytteltons Atelier arbeiten wollten, blieben oft gleich mehrere Wochen oder sogar Monate. Und das kann man gut verstehen. Die Gegend ist zwar sehr abgeschieden und im Winter kann viel Schnee fallen, aber die entspannte Atmosphäre des Hauses macht es den Besucher schwer, wieder abzureisen.

Unten: Celia wurde leidenschaftliche Sammlerin von Trödel, sie säuberte und restaurierte mühsam, aber begeistert einen langen Tapeziertisch und Essstühle aus Buchenholz, die sie in dem verlassenen Haus entdeckt hatte.

Facing page: Celia's etching studio was converted from the old weavers' barn. The northern light casts its cool eye on works in progress, including landscapes inspired by a trip to Yemen.
Above and right: The art of renovation, according to Celia, is to know when to stop. She loved the mottled plaster on the walls and considered recoloring and replastering carefully and with great respect for the originals. The patchwork bed quilt and draperies were all vintage.

Page de gauche: La vieille grange des tisserands a été convertie en atelier de gravure pour Celia. La lumière du Nord pose son regard froid sur les œuvres en cours, dont des paysages inspirés par un voyage au Yémen.
Ci-dessus et à droite: Selon Celia, tout l'art de la restauration consiste à savoir quand s'arrêter. Aimant les effets chatoyants du vieux plâtre sur les murs, elle a soigneusement étudié les couleurs avant de les enduire à neuf avec un grand respect pour les teintes d'origine. Le couvre-lit en patchwork et les rideaux sont des tissus anciens.

Linke Seite: Celias Atelier war früher die Scheune der Weber. Das Nordlicht wirft einen kühlen Blick auf ihre Arbeiten, zu denen auch Landschaften gehören, die unter dem Eindruck einer Reise in den Jemen entstanden.
Oben und rechts: Nach Meinung von Celia liegt die Kunst der Renovierung darin zu wissen, wann es genug ist. Sie liebt den fleckigen Putz an den Wänden. Deshalb war sie sehr vorsichtig, als die Wände neu verputzt und gestrichen wurden. Der Patchworkquilt und die Vorhänge sind alt.

Susanne and Olaf Rohwedder

Witzwort, Schleswig-Holstein, Germany

L'architecte Olaf Rohwedder est spécialisé dans la restauration de ces chaumières si typiques que l'on construit depuis des siècles dans le nord de l'Allemagne, près de la frontière danoise. Ces maisons aux façades blanchies à la chaux et aux robustes toits en jonc parsèment les basses terres tout le long du magnifique littoral de la mer du Nord. Elles forment une présence noble et graphique dans ces paysages de marais salants asséchés, d'îles fouettées par les tempêtes et de grandes marées. Olaf, sa femme Susanne et leurs enfants Carsten et Gothia habitent dans une de ces chaumières, construite en 1820. Celles-ci présentent un inconvénient, explique Rohwedder: elles ont traditionnellement de petites fenêtres qui rendent les intérieurs sombres. C'est pourquoi il a fait bâtir un jardin d'hiver près de leur étang, à 20 mètres de leur maison. Ses murs en briques recyclées et son toit en verre soutenu par une structure en aluminium ont été fabriqués par la firme anglaise Alitex. «En été, on y donne des fêtes. Tout au long de l'année, on y fait pousser des tomates, des capucines et des figuiers», confie Olaf.

Architect Olaf Rohwedder specializes in restoring the distinctive thatched houses that have been built for centuries in Northern Germany, near the Danish border. These whitewashed houses with their sturdy rush roofs dot the low-lying landscapes along the magnificent North Sea coast, and are a noble, graphic presence in this land of reclaimed salt marshes, storm-lashed islands, and high tides. Rohwedder, his wife, Susanne, son, Carsten, and daughter, Gothia, live in a thatched cottage dating back to 1820. Thatched houses have just one disadvantage, said Rohwedder – windows are traditionally small and the interiors can be dark. His solution was to design a small light-filled glasshouse beside a pond just 65 feet from their residence. Its reclaimed brick walls and aluminum-framed glass roof were built by the British firm, Alitex. "We give parties under glass in summer, and grow tomatoes, nasturtiums, and fig trees year-round," Olaf said.

Der Architekt Olaf Rohwedder hat sich auf die Renovierung von reetgedeckten Häusern spezialisiert, wie sie über Jahrhunderte hinweg in Norddeutschland nahe der dänischen Grenze gebaut wurden. Überall in der tief gelegenen Landschaft entlang der Nordseeküste verstreut, sind die weiß getünchten Häuser mit ihren dicken Strohdächern charakteristisch für die trockengelegten Marschgebiete und die windumtosten Inseln, die vom Wechsel der Gezeiten geprägt werden. Rohwedder lebt mit seiner Frau Susanne und den Kindern Carsten und Gothia in einem reetdeckten Landhaus von 1820. »Häuser mit Reetdach haben nur einen einzigen Nachteil«, meint Olaf Rohwedder; »Sie haben normalerweise sehr kleine Fenster, so dass es innen ziemlich dunkel ist.« Seine Lösung bestand darin, zusätzlich ein kleines lichtdurchflutetes Glashaus aufzustellen, das nur 20 Meter von dem Wohnhaus entfernt direkt neben einem kleinen Teich liegt. Das Glashäuschen verfügt über Wände aus alten Ziegelsteinen und ein Glasdach mit Aluminiumrahmen und wurde von der britischen Firma Alitex gebaut. »Im Sommer geben wir hier Partys und wir züchten das ganze Jahr über Tomaten, Kapuzinerkresse und Feigenbäume«, erzählt Olaf Rohwedder.

Carsten and Gothia Rohwedder feed their pet geese
on the bridge leading to the family's glasshouse, designed by their father. The pond is stocked with Japanese koi, and friendly trout.

Carsten et Gothia Rohwedder nourrissent leurs oies ap-
privoisées depuis le petit pont qui mène au jardin d'hiver de la famille, conçu par leur père. L'étang abrite
des kois japonais et de sympathiques truites.

Carsten und Gothia Rohwedder auf der Brücke, die zu
dem Glashaus führt, beim Füttern ihrer zahmen
Gänse. Im Teich wurden Koi, japanische Karpfen, und
Forellen eingesetzt.

The interior of the Rohwedders' glasshouse, with its salvaged sand-
stone floor, iron stove, and bricks reclaimed from dismantled old
buildings, is ideal for plant propagation. Teak benches and chairs invite rest and family gatherings in the evening around the stove. An
automatic temperature-control system opens and closes vents in the
glass roof to modulate the temperature.

Le jardin d'hiver des Rohwedder, avec son sol en dalles de grès, son
poêle en fonte et ses briques, le tout récupéré dans des bâtiments anciens en démolition, est idéal pour la reproduction des plantes. Des
bancs et des chaises en teck invitent au repos et aux réunions de famille le soir autour du feu. Un système automatique de contrôle de la
température ouvre des trappes dans la verrière s'il fait trop chaud.

In Olaf Rohwedders Glashaus. Es verfügt über einen Fußboden aus
wieder verwendetem Sandstein, einen gusseisernen Ofen und Ziegel-
steine, die aus verfallenen oder abgerissenen Häusern stammen. Im
Innern herrschen ideale Bedingungen für alle möglichen Pflanzenar-
ten. Die Familie sitzt gerne abends auf den Bänken und Stühlen aus
Teakholz um den Ofen. Eine automatische Temperaturregulierung
öffnet und schließt die Entlüftungsschlitze.

Witzwort, Schleswig-Holstein, Germany   Susanne and Olaf Rohwedder

Richtje and Matthijs Zeelenberg

Ouddorp, South Holland, the Netherlands

Pour la famille Zeelenberg, cette petite cabane de jardin posée au beau milieu des champs près de la mer vaut toutes les chambres avec vue. Le décorateur Piet Hein Eek a réalisé ce cabanon sur mesure en recyclant des planches de bois, des feuilles de zinc provenant de toits, un vieux parquet en chêne et des éléments d'architecture condamnés à la casse. «Les hautes fenêtres, principal élément de design, viennent d'un vieil hôpital. Le reste a été fait avec du bois de récupération», explique Eek dont les bureaux se trouvent à Geldrop, près d'Eindhoven aux Pays-Bas. «Je l'ai conçue de sorte à ce qu'elle puisse être préfabriquée, transportée sur un site et assemblée rapidement». Le mobilier est minimaliste – rien qu'une table et des bancs en bois. Eek a commencé à fabriquer ces maisonnettes pour un projet artistique. Devant leur succès, sa société, Eek en Ruijgrok, a pu se lancer dans des travaux encore plus ambitieux. «Quand vous créez des choses que vous aimez, les commanditaires vous laissent plus facilement carte blanche pour de nouveaux projets», observe Eek.

For the Zeelenberg family, a portable garden house set in the open fields near the coast is truly a room with a view. Interior designer Piet Hein Eek custom-crafted this one-of-a-kind pavilion using recycled woods, zinc roof panels, an old oak parquet floor, and salvaged architectural throw-aways. "The large windows, which are the most important design element, were originally part of an old hospital building. The rest of the pavilion was made from scrap wood," said Eek, whose design office is in Geldrop near Eindhoven in the Netherlands. "I designed it so that it can be prefabricated, taken to a site, and quickly put together." Furniture is minimal – just a little table and wood benches. Eek first started making these small houses as an art project. Their success paved the way for even more ambitious work for his company, Eek en Ruijgrok. "If you design what you love, you get more freedom for other creative commissions," Eek noted.

Zimmer mit Aussicht: So könnte man das leicht zu transportierende Gartenhäuschen der Familie Zeelenberg beschreiben, das nicht weit entfernt vom Meer auf dem freien Feld steht. Der Interior-Designer Piet Hein Eek stellte diesen Pavillon als Einzelstück in Maßanfertigung her; er verwendete dabei altes Holz, Dachverkleidungen aus Zink, einen alten Eichenparkettboden und weitere Elemente, die schon in anderen Häusern zum Einsatz gekommen waren. »Die großen Fenster sind das wichtigste Stilelement, früher gehörten sie zu einem Krankenhaus. Ansonsten haben wir Holzabfälle verwendet«, erzählt Eek, der ein Designbüro in Geldrop bei Eindhoven hat. »Ich habe den Entwurf so gestaltet, dass man für ihn Fertigteile verwenden kann, die man dann an den gewünschten Platz transportiert und dort einfach und schnell zusammensetzt.« Die Einrichtung ist minimalistisch – nur ein kleiner Tisch und Holzbänke. Am Anfang baute Eek seine kleinen Gartenhäuschen als Kunstprojekt, doch der Erfolg ebnete für Eek en Ruijgrok den Weg zu umfangreicheren Arbeiten. »Wenn man das designt, was man liebt, gewinnt man mehr kreative Freiheit bei anderen Aufträgen«, bemerkt Eek.

Ans Bakker

Dieren, the Veluwe, the Netherlands

Etait-ce la chance ou la réalisation d'un vœu pieux? Toujours est-il que l'artiste Ans Bakker a déniché la maison de ses rêves près d'Arnhem. Heureusement, elle était abandonnée mais sur le point d'être livrée aux démolisseurs. Elle vola aussitôt à sa rescousse. Armée de son nom de plume «Truusje Stoter», ce drôle d'oiseau squatta la bâtisse qu'elle transforma rapidement en son premier «nid douillet». Le squat est un phénomène assez répandu aux Pays-Bas mais Ans tenait à légaliser rapidement sa situation, ce qui advint après de nombreuses tasses de thé avec les voisins et l'aimable autorisation des autorités du village. La maison n'attendait qu'à renaître de ces cendres. Surmontée d'un étage, elle est entièrement en bois, avec un toit en tuiles de terre cuite. Ans a lessivé les pièces vides, restauré le vieux poêle à charbon, peint les murs et les plafonds en blanc et aménagé un jardin dans lequel elle peut se prélasser les soirs d'été.

Call it luck or fate or wishful thinking: artist Ans Bakker found the house of her dreams near Arnhem. The good news was that it wasn't actually occupied. But when she expressed an interest in the abandoned cottage, Ans soon discovered that there was talk of demolishing it. Ans to the rescue. Using "Truusje Stoter" as her nom de plume – more on feathers later – Ans squatted in the house, and turned it into her first "Bird's Nest". Squatting is not a rare phenomenon in the Netherlands, but Ans quickly and politely moved to make her residence official. With cups of tea for the neighbors and eventually with the approval of the village authorities, Ans became legal. It was a dream cottage – waiting to happen. The two-storey cottage is entirely made of wood, with a terracotta tile roof. She cleaned the empty rooms and restored an old coal stove, painted walls and ceilings white, and planted a garden so that she can sit outside on summer evenings.

Man kann es Glück nennen oder Schicksal oder auch Wunschdenken: Die Künstlerin Ans Bakker fand ihr Traumhaus in der Nähe von Arnheim. Ein Vorteil war, dass das Haus nicht bewohnt war. Aber als sie Interesse an dem verlassenen Gebäude zeigte, stellte sie schnell fest, dass es eigentlich abgerissen werden sollte. Doch man hatte nicht mit Ans gerechnet. Unter ihrem Künstlernamen Truusje Stoter besetzte sie das Haus und machte daraus ihr erstes eigenes Heim. Hausbesetzer sind in den Niederlanden keine Seltenheit, aber Ans ging schnell und entschlossen daran, ihren Aufenthalt zu legalisieren. Mit einigen Tassen Tee für die Nachbarn und schließlich der Genehmigung der Stadtbehörden erreichte sie ihr Ziel. Es war ein Traum-Cottage – allerdings im Dornröschenschlaf. Das zweigeschossige Haus ist vollständig aus Holz errichtet und ist mit Terrakottaziegeln gedeckt. Ans machte sich zuerst daran, die leeren Zimmer zu säubern, danach brachte sie den alten Kohleofen wieder in Gang, strich Wände und Decken weiß und legte einen Garten an, in dem sie nun die Sommerabende verbringt.

Left: Artist, theatrical designer, and party decorator Ans Bakker uses the rooms of her cottage as an experimental stage, improvising sets and weaving fantasies. Teak garden chairs with boldly striped upholstery are given dizzy silk draperies, and metamorphose into a celebration of ruffles and flourishes.
Facing page: The board and batten walls and the pine floor were given quick coats of paint to lighten the interiors. Boldly delineated flea market furniture with the look of heirlooms add a feeling of architecture to the simple rooms. A bird's nest chandelier forms a crown above the table.

A gauche: Artiste, décoratrice de théâtre et de fêtes, Ans Bakker utilise les pièces de son cottage comme une scène expérimentale, improvisant des décors et tissant des rêves. Des fauteuils de jardin en teck, recouverts de coussins aux rayures tranchées et encadrés d'étourdissantes draperies de soie, se métamorphosent en trônes d'apparat.
Page de droite: Les lambris en bois brut et le plancher en sapin ont été badigeonnés de plusieurs couches de peinture pour éclaircir les intérieurs. Les meubles chinés aux Puces semblent être des souvenirs de famille et confèrent de la grandeur aux pièces sobres. Un lustre nid forme une couronne au-dessus de la table.

Links: Die Künstlerin, Bühnenbildnerin und Party-Dekorateurin Ans Bakker lässt ihrer Fantasie freien Lauf und nutzt die Zimmer ihres Cottage als Experimentierbühne für improvisierte Szenarien. Über Gartenstühlen aus Teakholz mit kühn gestreiften Polsterbezügen bauschen sich Schwindel erregend glitzernde Seidenstoffe in prachtvollverschwenderischem Faltenwurf.
Rechte Seite: Die holzverschalten Wände und der Boden aus Kiefernholz wurden mit mehreren Farbschichten gestrichen, um das Haus innen heller erscheinen zu lassen. Kühn geschwungene Möbel vom Flohmarkt, die wie alte Familienerbstücke wirken, geben den schlichten Räumen architektonisches Flair. Ein Leuchter in Form eines Vogelnestes hängt wie eine Krone über dem Tisch.

Previous pages: Artist Ans Bakker's house was once the residence of municipal bus drivers and their families. She discovered it in a garden adjacent to a bus yard, in a small village just a hop and a skip from the city of Arnhem. Ans crafts fantasy decorations using feathers and crystals, glass beads and glittering found objects.
Right: Once the allure of feathers became all too apparent to Ans, she found a source for her collections at the local poulterer. Now she gathers them in vintage chests, ready for a flight of fancy.

Doubles pages précédentes: La maison de l'artiste Ans Bakker était autrefois un logement de fonction pour les chauffeurs de bus municipaux et leurs familles. Elle l'a découverte au fond d'un jardin jouxtant le parking des bus, dans un petit village situé à un jet de pierre de la ville d'Arnhem. Ans crée des décors oniriques à l'aide de plumes, de verreries de perles et de n'importe quel objet trouvé pourvu qu'il brille.
A droite: Séduite par l'élégance naturelle de la plume, Ans s'approvisionne chez son marchand de volailles local. Elle conserve ses collections dans de vieux coffres, en attendant que son imagination s'envole.

Vorhergehende Doppelseiten: Früher wohnten die Busfahrer des Orts mit ihren Familien in dem Haus, das jetzt der Künstlerin Ans Bakker gehört. Sie entdeckte es in einem Garten neben einem Busdepot in einem kleinen Dorf, nur einen Katzensprung von Arnheim entfernt. Ans verwendet für ihre fantasievollen Objekte Federn und Kristall, Glasperlen und glitzernde Fundstücke.
Rechts: Als Ans sich für Vogelfedern zu begeistern begann, wandte sie sich an den Geflügelhändler des Orts. Heute sammelt sie die Federn in alten Kisten, wo sie darauf warten, dass Ans' Fantasie ihnen Flügel verleiht.

Facing page: The daybed becomes a dreamy retreat, with lace-edged Belgian linen covers and ivory silken draperies with all the grace and drama of a Balenciaga ballgown. Birds and birds' nests became a motif, a creative exploration for Ans, who studied theatrical design.
Above and right: Ans can make even the simplest country bed into a palazzo of dreams.

Page de gauche: Le lit de repos, paré d'un dessus-de-lit bordé de dentelle belge, est devenu un refuge où rêver sous un baldaquin en soie ivoire qui a toute la grâce et l'allure d'une robe de bal de Balenciaga. Les oiseaux et leurs nids sont devenus un sujet d'inspiration et d'exploration créative pour Ans, qui a étudié la scénographie.
Ci-dessus et à droite: Ans sait transformer le moindre lit campagnard en couche de princesse de conte de fées.

Linke Seite: Das traumhafte Tagesbett mit einem spitzengesäumten belgischen Leinenüberwurf und einem elfenbeinfarbenen Baldachin aus Seide gleicht in seiner Anmut und Dramatik einem Ballkleid von Balenciaga. Vögel und Vogelnester wurden zum Leitmotiv und zu einer schöpferischen Herausforderung für Ans, die ausgebildete Bühnenbildnerin ist.
Oben und rechts: Selbst ein einfaches Landhausbett wird unter Ans' Händen zu einem Palast der Träume.

Above: In the four years since Ans discovered the cottage, her garden and imagination have flourished. Twig collages, honeysuckle and roses adorn the exterior.
Facing page: The kitchen is the only room with a straightforward, strictly functional nature. Painted and polished it is now a sunny breakfast spot.

Ci-dessus: Depuis quatre ans qu'elle habite ici, son jardin et son imagination se sont épanouis. Des collages de brindilles, du chèvrefeuille et des roses ornent la façade.
Page de droite: La cuisine est la seule pièce strictement fonctionnelle. Poncée et repeinte, c'est le lieu idéal pour prendre son petit déjeuner au soleil.

Oben: In den vier Jahren, seit Ans das Cottage entdeckt hat, erblühte der fantasievolle Garten in voller Pracht. Collagen aus Zweigen, rankendem Geißblatt und Rosen zieren die Außenwände.
Rechte Seite: Die Küche ist als einziges Zimmer vorwiegend funktionell gestaltet. Frisch gestrichen und sonnig, ist sie jetzt ein idealer Ort zum Frühstücken.

Marja Maassen and Jan Moereels

Brasschaat, Province of Antwerp, Belgium

C'est ce qu'on appelle avoir une vision verticale de la vie. Marja Maassen et Jan Moereels ont transformé un château d'eau abandonné du début du siècle en une élégante résidence hautement fonctionnelle. «Quand j'ai offert de racheter l'édifice pour en faire ma maison, tout le monde m'a ri au nez», se souvient Moereels qui est architecte paysagiste. La tour a été construite à titre privé entre 1900 et 1910 pour pomper, filtrer et stocker l'eau d'une rivière voisine afin d'approvisionner le château de Brasschaat et ses dépendances. Le parc de 85 hectares, appartenant aujourd'hui à la municipalité, était une réserve de chasse au cerf et au faisan très prisée. Avec ses 24 mètres de hauteur, la tour, l'un des premiers bâtiments industriels en béton de la région d'Anvers, domine la cime des arbres. Elle a cessé de fonctionner en 1937. Moereels l'a achetée en 1991 et a demandé aux architectes Jo Crepain et Dirk Engelen de la réaménager. «Nous avons examiné au moins 20 plans différents» se rappelle-t-il. La carcasse de béton a reçu une peau neuve en verre industriel transparent et opaque, ainsi qu'une nouvelle vie.

This is vertical living at its most dramatic. Marja Maassen and Jan Moereels have transformed a disused turn-of-the-century water tower into a glamorous and highly functional residence. "When I proposed purchasing the tower and making it my home, everyone laughed," said Moereels, a landscape architect. The tower was privately built between 1900 and 1910, to pump, filter and store water from a nearby river for Brasschaat Castle and its guest houses. The 170-acre country park, now town property, was a favorite haunt for hunting deer and pheasant. The 80-feet-tall tower, one of the first concrete industrial buildings in the Antwerp region, became obsolete in 1937. Moereels acquired it in 1991, and engaged architects Jo Crepain and Dirk Engelen to revive and transform the treetop-tall tower. "We went through at least 20 plans," recalled Moereels. The skeleton was given a skin of transparent and opaque industrial glass – and a new life.

Leben in der Vertikale in seiner kühnsten Form: Marja Maassen und Jan Moereels machten aus einem nicht mehr genutzten Wasserturm aus der Jahrhundertwende einen außergewöhnlichen und höchst funktionellen Wohnsitz. »Als ich die Idee hatte, den Turm zu kaufen und zu meiner Wohnung umzubauen, lachten alle nur«, erinnert sich der Landschaftsarchitekt Moereels heute. Der Turm wurde ursprünglich zwischen 1900 und 1910 privat errichtet, um Wasser aus einem nahe gelegenen Fluß abzupumpen, zu filtern und für Schloss Brasschaat zu speichern. Die etwa 700 000 Quadratmeter große Parkanlage, jetzt im Besitz der Stadt, war früher ein beliebtes Revier für die Rotwild- und Fasanenjagd. Der Turm, 24 Meter hoch und einer der ersten Industriebauten aus Beton in der Antwerpener Gegend, ist seit 1937 nicht mehr im Betrieb. Moereels erwarb 1991 den Turm, der bis zu den Baumwipfeln reicht, und beauftragte die Architekten Jo Crepain und Dirk Engelen mit dem Umbau. »Wir haben mindestens 20 verschiedene Baupläne besprochen und wieder verworfen«, erzählt Moereels. Schließlich beschlossen sie, dem Gebäude eine Haut aus transparentem und opakem Industrieglas überzuziehen und es darin zu neuem Leben zu erwecken.

Left and below: *Landscape designer Jan Moereels did much of the labor on the tower himself, pouring concrete and crafting the cherrywood and galvanized steel dining table, and the cherrywood bed and cabinets.*
Facing page: *Work on the tower took about two years. "It has a great feeling because it is open and light and spacious," noted Moereels. "You're in direct contact with nature. We're surrounded by birch, beech, and oak trees which demonstrate the passing seasons every day." A monolithic cherry kitchen counter is used for both dining and food preparation.*

A gauche et ci-dessous: *Architecte paysagiste, Jan Moereels a fait le plus gros des travaux lui-même, déversant le béton et réalisant la table en cerisier et acier galvanisé, ainsi que le lit et la bibliothèque en cerisier.*
Page de droite: *La tour est restée en travaux pendant deux ans. «On y est formidablement bien parce qu'elle est ouverte, claire et spacieuse», confie Moereels. «On est en contact direct avec la nature. Tout autour de nous, les bouleaux, les hêtres et les chênes illustrent chaque jour le passage des saisons». Le comptoir de cuisine monolithique en cerisier sert à la fois de table de salle à manger et de plan de travail pour préparer les repas.*

Links und unten: *Der Landschaftsarchitekt Jan Moereels führte viele Arbeiten an dem Turm selbst aus: Er goss Beton, zimmerte den Esstisch aus Kirschholz und galvanisiertem Stahl und fertigte auch die Betten und Schränke aus Kirschholz.*
Rechte Seite: *Die Arbeiten an dem Turm dauerten etwa zwei Jahre. »Es ist ein tolles Gefühl, hier zu leben, denn alles ist offen, hell und großzügig«, bemerkt Moereels. »Dazu kommt der direkte Kontakt zur Natur. Wir schauen direkt auf Birken, Buchen und Eichen und erleben die Jahreszeiten hautnah mit.« Eine monumentale Kirschholztheke dient gleichzeitig als Esstisch und Arbeitsplatte.*

First pages: *On the ground floor of the Moereels tower are a minimalist kitchen, living room and entryway. Above it, facing into the woods, are bathrooms and a study, and above them floats a bedroom. There is a guest bedroom in a monastic space with a simple painted bed and a steel gangway up to the winter garden. The tower is heated in winter with gas and a floor heating system. From the top of the tower, the family can see Antwerp, six miles away.*
Previous pages: *The white sofa in the living room is "Throwaway" by Zanotta. A pair of chairs were designed by Poul Kjaerholm.*

Premières pages: *Le rez-de-chaussée accueille un vestibule, une cuisine minimaliste et un salon. Au deuxième niveau, face à la forêt, se trouvent les salles de bains et un bureau, au-dessus desquels flotte une chambre à coucher. Une chambre d'ami monacale avec un simple lit peint et une passerelle en acier menant au jardin d'hiver. En hiver, la tour est chauffée au gaz et par un système de chauffage par le sol. Du haut de sa tour, on peut voir Anvers, située à dix kilomètres.*
Double page précédente: *Le canapé blanc est un «Jetable» de Zanotta. La paire de chaises a été dessinée par Poul Kjaerholm.*

Eingangsseiten: *Im Erdgeschoss des Turms befinden sich eine minimalistisch eingerichtete Küche, ein Wohnzimmer und der Eingangsbereich. Darüber, mit Blick in die Bäume, liegen die Badezimmer und ein Arbeitszimmer, ganz oben ein Schlafzimmer. Vom asketisch wirkenden Gästezimmer mit dem schlichten bemalten Bett führt eine Stahlleiter hinauf in den Wintergarten. Im Winter wird der Turm mit Gas und einer Fußbodenheizung beheizt. Von der Turmspitze aus sieht die Familie auf das 10 Kilometer entfernte Antwerpen.*
Vorhergehende Doppelseite: *Das weiße Sofa »Throwaway« im Wohnzimmer ist von Zanotta. Die beiden Stühle sind Entwürfe von Poul Kjaerholm.*

Annick Argant and Jean-Claude Le Marchand

Ile de Bréhat, Brittany, France

C'est un conte de fées classique sur une île magique. Jean-Claude Le Marchand et Annick Argant, tous deux artistes, vivent sur une île rocailleuse de la Manche qui fait tout juste trois kilomètres de long, dans une maison qui semble avoir été dessinée par un enfant. Bien que construite dans les années 1920 par le grand-père de Jean-Claude, elle paraît toute jeune et pleine de vie grâce à la créativité bouillonnante et à l'humour excentrique de ses occupants. Ils ont réaménagé l'intérieur, l'ont habillé de miroirs et de meubles recyclés, puis l'ont peuplé d'étranges petits personnages créés à partir d'objets trouvés par Annick. Lorsqu'ils ne sont pas occupés à transformer leurs rêves en réalité à grands renforts de pastels, d'huiles et d'argile, ils arpentent leur île, ses ruines gallo-romaines, ses phares robustes, ses chapelles en pierres et ses promontoires rocheux d'où l'on peut admirer la mer translucide. Bréhat est connue pour Birlot, un moulin à marée construit sur la grève entre 1633 et 1638. Elle abrite également des cormorans, des hérons, des mouettes à tête noire et les fantômes de corsaires d'antan.

It's a classic fairy tale on a magical island. Artists Jean-Claude Le Marchand and his wife, Annick Argant, live in a child's drawing of a house on a rocky English Channel island that's just two miles long. Jean-Claude's grandfather built the house in the far-distant 1920s, but the house today looks young and full of life, thanks to the restless creative spirits and quirky humor of the owners. They refurbished the house, dressed it with painted mirrors and recycled furniture, and gave it a cast of droll characters created from found objects by Annick. And when they are not bringing their dreams to life in pastels and oils and clay, they roam their island, past Gallo-Roman ruins, sturdy lighthouses and stone chapels, and from translucent channels to rocky outcrops. Bréhat is famous for the Birlot tide mill, constructed on the shore between 1633 and 1638. And it's home to cormorants, herons, black-headed gulls and the ghosts of long-ago pirates.

Wie ein Märchen auf einer Zauberinsel: Die Künstler Jean-Claude Le Marchand und seine Frau Annick Argant leben mitten im Ärmelkanal auf einer Felseninsel, die gerade mal drei Kilometer lang ist. Ihr Haus sieht aus wie eine Kinderzeichnung, Jean-Claudes Großvater hat es bereits in den 1920er-Jahren erbaut, aber es ist immer noch frisch und voller Leben. Mit viel Kreativität und Humor renovierten Jean-Claude und seine Frau ihr Haus, richteten es mit alten Möbeln ein und dekorierten es mit bemalten Spiegeln sowie liebenswerten witzigen Figuren, die Annick aus Fundstücken fertigt. Wenn sie nicht gerade ihre Träume in Pastell, Öl oder Ton zum Leben erwecken, dann durchstreifen sie »ihre« Insel, vorbei an gallorömischen Ruinen, aufragenden Leuchttürmen, steinernen Kapellen, schimmernden Kanälen und wilden Felsvorsprüngen. Die Insel Bréhat ist berühmt für die Gezeitenmühle von Birlot, die zwischen 1633 und 1638 an der Küste gebaut wurde, und sie ist auch Heimat für Kormorane, Reiher, Schwarzkopfmöwen und natürlich die Geister der Korsaren, die früher hier ihr Unwesen trieben.

First pages: *Jean-Claude Le Marchand takes a break in the sunshine in front of their house, in L'Allégöat, on Ile de Bréhat. He and Annick Argant announce the hours of opening for their studio on the gate, and welcome visitors to visit and chat. In the kitchen are Jean-Claude's pastels, and hearty heirloom furniture they have painted.*
Above, right and facing page: *Even the bathrooms are a canvas for the artists' expression. Arabesques of gold paint ornament the frosted glass door. Above the wash basin, a large square mirror is decorated with silhouettes of Breton women in their traditional coiffs.*

Premières pages: *Jean-Claude Le Marchand prend le soleil devant sa maison, à l'Allégöat sur l'île de Bréhat. Sur le portail sont annoncées les heures d'ouverture de l'atelier. Dans la cuisine, des pastels de Jean-Claude et des meubles de famille repeints par le couple.*
Ci-dessus, à droite et page de droite: *Des arabesques dorées ornent les vitres en verre dépoli. Au-dessus du lavabo, un grand miroir carré est décoré de silhouettes de Bretonnes coiffées de bigoudènes.*

Eingangsseiten: *Jean-Claude Le Marchand genießt die Sonnenstrahlen vor seinem Haus in L'Allégöat auf der Ile de Bréhat. Am Gartentor sind die Öffnungszeiten des Ateliers angeschlagen. Besucher sind herzlich willkommen. Die Küche schmücken Jean-Claudes Pastellbilder und alte Möbel, Familienerbstücke, die sie neu bemalt haben.*
Oben, rechts und rechte Seite: *Auch in den Badezimmern waren Annick und Jean-Claude kreativ: Goldene Arabesken schmücken die Milchglasscheiben der Tür. Den Spiegel über dem Waschbecken zieren Silhouetten von bretonischen Frauen mit ihren typischen hohen Hauben.*

Ile de Bréhat, Brittany, France   Annick Argant and Jean-Claude Le Marchand

Catherine and Jean-Patrick Razon

Ile d'Ouessant, Brittany, France

Sur la carte, l'île d'Ouessant, souvent appelée la terre la plus occidentale de l'Europe, ressemble à un gros rocher qui se serait détaché de la pointe de la Bretagne pour s'aventurer dans l'océan Atlantique. Fouettées par les vagues, ses côtes déchiquetées lui confèrent un air d'indépendance et de courage, tenant fièrement tête aux tempêtes et aux épais brouillards qui descendent de la Manche et de la mer d'Irlande. Les maisons en pierres, typiques de cette île qui ne compte que 932 habitants, sont blotties les unes contre les autres et semblent avoir jailli spontanément de la roche. Les Razon sont tombés amoureux d'une vieille ferme située non loin du phare du Stiff. Jean-Patrick, un ethnologue qui a étudié les Indiens d'Amazonie, et Catherine, une illustratrice, ont toujours été convaincus que leur maison tenait son âme des vies passionnées qui s'y sont succédées au fil des siècles. L'intérieur, traversé par un grand hamac sud-américain multicolore, est un vaste espace ouvert où dominent les textures riches du granit et du vieux sapin.

On a map, the rocky island of Ouessant, often called the western edge of Europe, looks like a chunk of land that broke off the tip of Brittany and ventured out into the Atlantic Ocean. Lashed by waves and rough-edged, it has an air of independence and grit, a proud sense of surviving the gales and fogs that blast south from the English Channel and the Celtic Sea. Traditional stone houses on the island, population 932, cluster and cling together for protection, and seem to have grown out of the stone outcrops. Catherine and Jean-Patrick – she is an illustrator, and he is an ethnologist who has studied the Indians of the Amazon – fell in love with an old farmhouse not far from the Stiff lighthouse. They have always felt their house has a spirit, a feeling of passionate lives lived there for hundreds of years. The interior, caparisoned with a large, colorful South American hammock, is one vast open space rich with the textures of granite and old pine.

Auf einer Landkarte wirkt die felsige Insel Ouessant, die auch als westlichste Ecke Europas bezeichnet wird, wie ein Stück Land, das von der Spitze der Bretagne abgebrochen ist und sich nun in den Atlantik vorwagt. Die wellenumtoste, raue Insel vermittelt eine Aura von Unabhängigkeit, von dem stolzen Gefühl, den Stürmen und Nebeln zu trotzen, die vom Ärmelkanal und der Irischen See südwärts ziehen. Die traditionellen Steinhäuser der 932 Einwohner drängen sich Schutz suchend aneinander und scheinen direkt den Felsen entwachsen zu sein. Die Illustratorin Catherine Razon und ihr Mann Jean-Patrick, ein Ethnologe, der am Amazonas indianische Kulturen erforscht hat, verliebten sich in ein altes Haus nicht weit entfernt vom Leuchtturm Phare du Stiff. Sie sind beide überzeugt davon, dass ihr Haus ein ganz eigenes Wesen hat und die Geister derjenigen, die hier über die Jahrhunderte gelebt haben, immer noch spürbar sind. Im Innern überspannt eine farbenprächtige Hängematte aus Südamerika den großen offenen Raum, der von den Materialien Granit und Kiefernholz beherrscht wird.

A Restored Farmhouse

Normandy, France

Partir à l'aventure en Normandie au printemps et en été offre la plus délicieuse des escapades. La moindre parcelle de nourriture déposée sur la table du petit déjeuner, du déjeuner et du dîner sent l'épaisse crème fraîchement barattée, le beurre doré qui fleure bon l'herbe, les fromages onctueux et le lait parfumé aux boutons d'or. Des vaches couleur crème paissent dans des prés luxuriants, débordantes de santé et de satisfaction. Les douces collines normandes parsemées de bosquets forment un puzzle de champs fraîchement labourés, de haies en fleurs et de prairies où perle la rosée, le tout encadré de forêts ancestrales. Peut-être est-ce le soleil se reflétant sur l'Atlantique voisin qui donne à la Normandie sa luminosité éclatante. Née sur cette terre bénie des dieux, l'antiquaire et décoratrice Françoise Piccino a restauré avec amour une ferme fortifiée vieille de sept siècles au sud de Deauville. La noble demeure et ses dépendances en schiste et granit ont été rénovées avec un grand respect des traditions architecturales de la région selon la devise: «Le moins fait le plus».

Adventuring through Normandy in the spring and summer is one of the most delicious diversions. Rich, freshly churned cream, grass-scented golden butter, unctuous cheeses, and milk that tastes of golden buttercups seem present in every morsel of nourishment set forth for breakfast, lunch and dinner. Cream-colored cows in lush meadows glow with health and contentment. Rolling Norman hills and bosky landscapes are a jigsaw puzzle of loamy ploughed fields, flowering hedgerows, and dew-fresh grasslands. Perhaps it is the sunshine reflected on the nearby Atlantic Ocean that gives Normandy its luminescent light. Antiques dealer and decorator Françoise Piccino was born here, and it was her great pleasure to restore this 700-year-old fortified farmhouse south of Deauville. The noble house and outbuildings of shale and granite were revived with great sensitivity to the building techniques of the region. "Less is more," was the mantra.

Im Frühling oder Sommer durch die Normandie zu fahren ist ein köstliches Vergnügen, denn zu jeder richtigen normannischen Mahlzeit gehören dicke, frisch geschlagene Sahne, nach Gras duftende goldfarbene Butter, kräftiger Käse und Milch, die nach gelben Butterblumen schmeckt. Sahnefarbene Kühe stehen auf saftigen Weiden und strotzen geradezu vor Gesundheit und Zufriedenheit. Die sanften Hügel der Normandie durchzieht ein Puzzle aus gepflügten Feldern, blühenden Hecken und taufrischem Grasland, alles eingerahmt von uralten Wäldern. Vielleicht beruht das Leuchten der Normandie darauf, dass der nahe gelegene Atlantik das Sonnenlicht reflektiert. Die Antiquitätenhändlerin und Dekorateurin Françoise Piccino stammt aus dieser gesegneten Landschaft und sie hat mit viel Freude ihr 700 Jahre altes, festungsartiges Bauernhaus südlich von Deauville restauriert. Bei dem Umbau griff sie auf traditionelle Bautechniken zurück und erweckte das prächtige Haus und seine Nebengebäude aus Schiefer und Granit mit viel Feingefühl zu neuem Leben. »Weniger ist mehr«, war ihr Leitmotiv.

Previous pages: To recreate a traditional-style interior, the walls were white-washed then applied with natural ocher for a golden, sunny look with a feeling of antiquity.
Above, right and facing page: The kitchen was updated, refreshed and restyled in a warm, traditional style to look as if it had not changed for centuries. In keeping with the rustic nature of the house, antique treasures are brought out for a summer repast.
Following pages: Hemp coverlets and linen sheets dress the bed.

Premières pages: Les murs ont été blanchis à la chaux puis teintés d'un ocre naturel pour obtenir un aspect doré et ensoleillé et leur donner un effet patiné par le temps.
Ci-dessus, à droite et page de droite: La cuisine a été modernisée et redécorée dans un style traditionnel chaleureux qu'on pourrait croire inchangé depuis des siècles. Conformément à la nature rustique de la maison, les trésors de famille ont été ressortis pour un festin d'été.
Double page suivante: Le lit est paré de draps en lin et d'un dessus-de-lit en chanvre ancien.

Vorhergehende Doppelseite: Um den Räumen ihren traditionellen Stil wiederzugeben, wurden die Wände zuerst weiß getüncht und dann mit einem natürlichen Ockerfarbton gestrichen, was ihnen einen goldenen, sonnigen Ton mit leicht antikem Anstrich verlieh.
Oben, rechts und rechte Seite: Die Küche wurde modernisiert und wirkt trotzdem, als hätte sich seit Jahrhunderten nichts verändert. Passend zur rustikalen Stimmung des Hauses wird auf altem Geschirr Traditionelles als sommerlicher Imbiss serviert.
Folgende Doppelseite: Hanfdecken und Laken bedecken das Bett.

Monique Germain

Vallée de Coulommiers,
Ile de France, France

Monique Germain n'oubliera jamais le jour où elle et son mari virent pour la première fois la ferme de Mussien. «C'était une vraie ruine, un triste spectacle, on en avait tous les deux les larmes aux yeux». L'élégante Mme Germain est admirée pour son salon de robes de mariées de la rive gauche à Paris. Le corps principal du bâtiment et les dépendances de la ferme, dont certaines parties remontent au 13e siècle, étaient rassemblés autour d'un vieux moulin. Située dans la vallée de Coulommiers, la ferme se trouvait sur la route des saints ordres des Templiers et était fréquentée par des fidèles de Sainte-Fare. «Selon les archives historiques, le moulin fournissait de la farine à un monastère voisin», raconte Mme Germain. «Nous sommes tombés amoureux de cette ferme parce qu'elle était si authentique, si pure. Elle n'avait pas été touchée depuis des décennies». Pour l'aménager, elle a fait appel au cabinet de Paul Mathieu et Michael Ray, qui ont su lui donner une atmosphère poétique, allusive, subtile et suggestive d'une vie de ferme éternelle.

Monique Germain vividly remembers the day when she and her husband first saw La Ferme de Mussien. "It was in total ruin, a sad sight, and we both had tears in our eyes," said Mme Germain. The chic Mme Germain is admired for her couture wedding salon, Monique Germain, on Paris's Left Bank. The cluster of unrestored farm buildings and a farmhouse, several of them dating back to the 13th century, had been built in the Coulommiers valley around an old mill. The region was on the routes of the holy orders of Templars, and popular with followers of Sainte Fare. "The original mill ground flour for monks of a nearby monastery, according to historical records," noted Mme Germain. "We loved the farm because it was so authentic, so pure. It had not been touched for decades." For her residence, Mme Germain engaged the firm of Paul Mathieu and Michael Ray. The result of their collaboration is poetic, subtle and suggestive of eternal farm life.

Monique Germain erinnert sich noch genau an den Tag, an dem sie und ihr Mann die Ferme de Mussien zum ersten Mal sahen. »Es war praktisch eine Ruine, ein trauriger Anblick, und wir hatten beide Tränen in den Augen«, sagt sie. Die elegante Monique besitzt eine Boutique für Hochzeitscouture am Rive Gauche in Paris. Das Bauernhaus und seine zahlreichen unrestaurierten Nebengebäude, von denen einige bis auf das 13. Jahrhundert zurückgehen, waren ursprünglich bei einer alten Mühle im Tal von Coulommiers errichtet worden. Diese Gegend lag direkt an den Pilgerstraßen der Tempelritter und wurde auch von den Anhängern der heiligen Fare benutzt. »Aus alten Urkunden geht hervor, dass früher in der Mühle Mehl für die Mönche eines nahe gelegenen Klosters gemahlen wurde«, erzählt Monique Germain. »Wir verliebten uns in dieses Haus, weil es so authentisch und unberührt war. Es war seit Jahrzehnten unverändert geblieben.« Sie beauftragte die Firma von Paul Mathieu und Michael Ray mit einer behutsamen Restaurierung. Das Ergebnis ist poetisch, subtil und voller Anspielungen auf das Leben auf dem Land.

Previous pages: The Ferme de Mussien is situated near the Aubetin river, in the Seine-et-Marne department.
Above and right: For the bedroom on the lower level, Mathieu and Ray shaped a bed from 13th-century columns and old timbers. It is used for naps, and children love to clamber on it. The series of turned-wood floor lamps, tables, and forged iron icons were all designed by the design duo. "Their color sense is superb," noted Monique Germain. "The pale cream walls add a wonderful emphasis to the old hand-hewn beams, the concrete floors and linen fabrics."

Double page précédente: La Ferme de Mussien est située sur les bords de l'Aubetin, en Seine-et-Marne.
Ci-dessus et à droite: Dans la chambre de l'étage inférieur, Mathieu et Ray ont façonné un lit à partir de colonnes du 13ᵉ siècle et de poutres anciennes. Il sert pour les siestes et les enfants adorent y grimper. La série de lampadaires et de tables en bois tourné ainsi que les icônes en fer forgé ont été dessinés par le tandem de designers. «Ils ont un magnifique sens de la couleur», observe Monique Germain. «Les murs beige pâle font merveilleusement ressortir les poutres artisanales, le sol en ciment et les tissus en lin».

Vorhergehende Doppelseite: Die Ferme de Mussien liegt nah beim Fluss Aubetin im Département Seine-et-Marne.
Oben und rechts: Im Schlafzimmer im Erdgeschoss steht ein Bett aus alten Balken und mit Säulen, die noch aus dem 13. Jahrhundert stammen. Es dient vor allem für Siestas und Kinder tollen gerne darin herum. Mehrere Stehlampen aus gedrechseltem Holz, Tische und schmiedeeiserne Objekte wurden von dem Designerduo selbst entworfen. »Die beiden besitzen einen fantastischen Sinn für Farben«, schwärmt Monique Germain. »Die zart cremefarbenen Wände bringen die alten Balken und die Leinenstoffe erst richtig zur Geltung.«

Vallée de Coulommiers, Ile de France, France   Monique Germain

Right: In the linen room, old pine cupboards were originally used to store sacks of flour. Here on the old oak plank floor, the family keeps heirloom linens and bedding.
Below: The pure and focused aesthetic of designers Michael Ray and Paul Mathieu is visible in the living room, with its monochromatic color scheme, sculptural furniture, and graceful lighting.

A droite: Dans la chambre à linge, les placards en vieux sapin servaient autrefois à entreposer les sacs de farine. C'est ici, sur le vieux plancher en chêne, que sont désormais rangés les draps de lin et la literie de famille.
Ci-dessous: Dans la salle de séjour à la palette monochrome, au mobilier sculptural et à l'éclairage délicat, on reconnaît l'esthétique épurée et concentrée de Michael Ray et de Paul Mathieu.

Rechts: In den alten Kiefernschränken im Wäschezimmer, in denen früher Mehlsäcke gestapelt wurden, bewahrt die Familie jetzt Erbstücke auf: alte Bettwäsche, Decken und Kissen.
Unten: Besonders im Wohnzimmer zeigt sich die puristische und auf einige wenige Objekte reduzierte Ästhetik der Designer Michael Ray und Paul Mathieu. Charakteristisch sind die monochrome Farbpalette, skulptural wirkende Einzelstücke und anmutige Lichteffekte.

A 17th Century Chartreuse

Périgord, France

Dans la vie, un vœu enfin exaucé apporte les plaisirs les plus doux. Le propriétaire de cette remarquable chartreuse la vit pour la première fois alors, qu'âgé de dix ans, il se promenait à cheval. Il tomba sous le charme des proportions classiques de la bâtisse séculaire et de la manière dont elle se fondait dans le paysage. Bien des années plus tard, elle devint sienne. Au début du printemps, lorsque les marronniers et les vieux chênes reviennent à la vie, la maison semble disparaître sous des nuages de feuillage vert. Restaurée par ce grand voyageur, elle accueille ses amis, ses fleurs, ses petits-enfants et des musiciens qui viennent y jouer. «Les plus belles maisons sont faites de larmes et de beaucoup d'amour» affirme son propriétaire avisé, tandis qu'il prend soin de ses roses. Il en a 120 espèces, principalement roses, jaunes et cramoisies. Il souligne que ses favorites sont la Maréchal Niel, Tuscany Superb, La Belle Sultane, New Dawn, Empereur du Maroc, York et Lancaster, et cueille des bouquets qu'il placera ensuite dans le grand salon et sa chambre.

In life, a longing fulfilled offers the sweetest pleasures. The owner of this remarkable chartreuse first saw his house when he was out riding, at the age of ten. He loved the way the centuries-old stone house was at home on the land, admired its classic proportions. Many years later, it was his. In early spring as chestnut trees and ancient oaks come to life, the house seems to disappear in clouds of green leaves. Restored by this world traveler, it becomes the stage for friends, flowers, adored grandchildren, and musicians who play in these handsome rooms. "The most beautiful houses are made out of tears and a lot of love," says the wise owner, as he plunges into beds of his 120 pampered roses, mostly pink, yellow and crimson. He appraises his favorites, *Maréchal Niel, Tuscany Superb, La Belle Sultane, New Dawn, Empereur de Maroc,* and *York et Lancaster,* and clips blooms to arrange in the grand salon and his bedroom.

Zu den schönsten Erlebnissen gehört es, wenn sich ein lang gehegter Wunsch endlich erfüllt. Der Besitzer dieses wunderschönen Hauses sah es zum ersten Mal bei einem Ausritt, als er gerade zehn Jahre alt war. Schon damals bewunderte er die klassischen Proportionen des jahrhundertealten Steinhauses und die Art, wie es sich in die Landschaft einfügte. Heute, viele Jahre später, gehört es ihm. In den ersten Frühlingstagen, wenn die Kastanienbäume und die alten Eichen wieder zum Leben erwachen, hüllt es sich in eine Wolke aus grünem Laub. Der Weltreisende renovierte das Haus und machte es zu einer Bühne für Freunde, Blumen, Enkelkinder und Musiker, die hier Konzerte geben. »Die schönsten Häuser sind aus Tränen und einer Menge Liebe gemacht«, sagt der Besitzer weise und verschwindet in seinen Rosenbeeten, in denen über 120 verschiedene, meist roséfarbene, gelbe und karmesinrote Rosen wachsen. Und während er von seinen Lieblingssorten erzählt, der Maréchal Niel, Tuscany Superb, La Belle Sultane, New Dawn, Empereur de Maroc und der York et Lancaster, schneidet er einige Blüten ab, um sie im großen Salon und seinem Schlafzimmer zu arrangieren.

Previous pages, above and right: In the 17th and 18th century, this chartreuse was built by French lesser nobles. Around one mile from the nearest town, it is surrounded by lime trees and a newly shaped garden.
Following pages: "With tall windows on all sides, the house is in effect a lantern," says the owner. In the music room, the biggest room in the house, he listens to the Goldberg Variations, pop music, movie themes. He restored the plaster walls using sand from the local river.

Premières pages, ci-dessus et à droite: Cette chartreuse fut construite aux 17ᵉ et 18ᵉ siècles par la petite noblesse française. Située à deux kilomètres de la ville la plus proche, elle est entourée de tilleuls et d'un jardin nouvellement redessiné.
Double page suivante: Percée de toutes parts de hautes fenêtres, la bâtisse est comme une lanterne, confie son propriétaire. Dans le salon de musique, la plus grande pièce de la maison, il écoute les variations Goldberg, de la pop et des musiques de films. Il a restauré les murs stuqués avec du sable de la rivière locale.

Vorhergehende Doppelseite, oben und rechte Seite: Dieses Landhaus wurde im 17. und 18. Jahrhundert von französischen Kleinadeligen erbaut. Das Haus ist zwei Kilometer von der nächsten Ortschaft entfernt und liegt umgeben von Limonenbäumen und einem neu angelegten Garten.
Folgende Doppelseite: »Mit den hohen Fenstern an allen Seiten gleicht das Haus einer Laterne«, meint der Besitzer. Im Musikzimmer, dem größten Raum des Hauses, hört er die Goldberg-Variationen, Pop- und Filmmusik. Für die Renovierung des Putzes verwendete er Sand aus dem nahe gelegenen Fluss.

Périgord, France · A 17th Century Chartreuse

The newly bestowed architecture of the house has a sense of austerity and understatement. It also looks original. Throughout the year, the owner immerses himself in traditional country pleasures; reading, rose-cultivation, antiques, roof-mending. "We were meant for each other, this house and I," he said. "It's elegant and rustic and simple."

L'architecture de la maison est austère et humble tout en étant raffinée. Tout au long de l'année, son propriétaire s'immerge dans les plaisirs simples de la campagne : lire, cultiver les roses, chiner des antiqui-tés et réparer le toit. «Cette maison et moi étions faits l'un pour l'autre» déclare-t-il. «Elle est élégante, rustique et simple».

Das vor kurzem restaurierte Gebäude vermittelt ein Gefühl von Schlichtheit und Understatement und wirkt gleichzeitig auch sehr authentisch. Das ganze Jahr über genießt der Besitzer die einfachen Vergnügen des Landlebens: Er liest, züchtet Rosen, sammelt Antiqui-täten und repariert das Dach. »Dieses Haus und ich – wir sind füreinander bestimmt. Es ist elegant und gleichzeitig rustikal und schlicht.«

Périgord, France

A 17th Century Chartreuse

Following pages: The floors were all redone in limestone, now covered with rush matting, as in the petit salon. Garden roses scent the air. The complex construction of the chestnut beams suggested to the owner that the craftsmen were former naval boat-builders from La Rochelle.

Double page suivante: Les sols ont tous été refaits en dalles anciennes et sont à présent recouverts de tapis de jonc, comme dans le petit salon. Les roses du jardin embaument. A en juger par la charpente complexe en poutres de noyer, le propriétaire pense que ses bâtisseurs étaient d'anciens ouvriers des chantiers navals de La Rochelle.

Folgende Doppelseite: In allen Räumen wurden Kalksteinplatten auf den Böden verlegt und – wie hier im kleinen Salon – mit Seegrasmatten bedeckt. Frisch geschnittene Rosen aus dem Garten verströmen ihren Duft. Die komplizierte Balkenkonstruktion aus Kastanienholz erinnert daran, dass das Haus von ehemaligen Schiffsbauern aus La Rochelle errichtet worden ist.

Capcazal de Pachiou

Mimbaste, Gascony, France

Les touristes qui se promènent dans Mimbaste, un village de la Chalosse, cette région verdoyante du sud-ouest de la France, marchent souvent sans le savoir sur les traces des Romains et empruntent le chemin des pèlerins qui, depuis des siècles, passent par ici en route vers Saint-Jacques de Compostelle. La Chalosse, avec ses océans de pinèdes et ses petites fermes perchées sur des collines, faisait autrefois partie de la riche province romaine d'Aquitania. Aujourd'hui encore, ce passé romantique est perceptible dans chaque clairière, chaque allée tortueuse et chaque ruisseau caillouteux. C'est une terre luxuriante riche en vignobles, en saints obscurs, en bains thermaux, en anciennes arènes et en musées de la préhistoire qui font la fierté de leurs municipalités. Le paisible Mimbaste, au sud-est de Dax, est niché au confluent boisé du Luy et du Grand Arrigan. Le village est entouré de moulins, de maisons de meuniers et de refuges de bergers perchés dans les collines. C'est aussi là que se trouve le remarquable Capcazal de Pachiou, le nec plus ultra de la retraite rustique.

Visitors wandering through the small town of Mimbaste, in the verdant Chalosse region of south-western France, often find themselves walking in the footsteps of the Romans, who set up camp here, and in the pathways of pilgrims who for centuries walked this way to Santiago de Compostela. Chalosse, with its oceans of old pine forests, and small hillside farms, was once part of rich Roman Aquitania. Still, today, a sense of the romantic past seems to cling to every clearing in the forest, every twisting lane and rocky stream. It's a green region of old vineyards, obscure saints, thermal baths, ancient arenas, and proudly arranged town museums of prehistory. Calm Mimbaste, south-east of Dax, is nestled at the leafy confluence of the Luy and Grand Arrigan rivers. Out on the edge of the village are mills and millers' cottages, shepherds' hillside refuges. Here, too, is the remarkable Capcazal de Pachiou, the ultimate rustic retreat.

In dem kleinen Dorf Mimbaste in der grünen Landschaft der Chalosse im Südwesten Frankreichs wandert man auf den Spuren der Römer, die hier ein Lager errichtet hatten, oder folgt alten Pilgerwegen, die seit vielen Jahrhunderten nach Santiago de Compostela führen. Die Chalosse mit ihren riesigen, uralten Pinienwäldern und kleinen, an den Hängen gelegenen Bauernhöfen gehörte in der Antike zur reichen römischen Provinz Aquitanien. Und noch heute scheint ein Hauch dieser romantischen Vergangenheit auf jeder Waldlichtung, jedem sich windenden Pfad oder Felsbach zu liegen. Es ist eine Region mit alten Weingärten, obskuren Lokalheiligen, Thermalbädern, antiken Arenen und Heimatmuseen, in denen voller Stolz prähistorische Fundstücke gezeigt werden. Das stille Dorf Mimbaste südöstlich von Dax schmiegt sich in die Wälder am Zusammenfluss der Luy und des Grand Arrigan. Am Rand des Dorfes liegen Mühlen und verlassene Müllerhäuser, heute Zufluchtsort für die Schafhirten. Und hier liegt auch das Landhaus Capcazal de Pachiou, der ultimative Rückzugsort auf dem Land.

Above, right, and facing page: *Finely-detailed wood paneling, old stone floors quarried nearby, and grand-scale rooms attest to the family's good fortune. Even the bronze doorknocker is original.*
Following pages: *The romantic bedrooms of the Capcazal de Pachiou offer time out of mind. Is this the 17th century or the 21st? The princely handcarved and gilded bed, carved stone fireplace, gilded mirrors and antique textiles await those with a desire to swoon – and sleep in late.*

Ci-dessus, à droite et page de droite: *Les boiseries finement sculptées, les vieux sols en dalles de pierres locales et les salons d'apparat témoignent de l'opulence des bâtisseurs des lieux. Même le heurtoir en bronze sur la porte est d'origine.*
Double page suivante: *Dans les chambres romantiques, on se sent hors du temps. Sommes-nous au 17ᵉ ou au 21ᵉ siècle? Le lit princier, sculpté et doré, la cheminée en pierre sculptée, les miroirs dorés et les étoffes anciennes attendent que l'on se pâme... et les amateurs de grasse matinée.*

Oben, rechts und rechte Seite: *Feingearbeitete Holzpaneele, alte Steinfußböden aus nahe gelegenen Steinbrüchen und die großzügigen Räume zeugen von Wohlstand. Sogar der Türklopfer aus Bronze ist ein Originalstück.*
Folgende Doppelseite: *In den romantischen Schlafzimmern verliert man jedes Zeitgefühl. Ist man im 17. oder im 21. Jahrhundert? Ein fürstliches, handgeschnitztes und vergoldetes Bett, ein Kamin mit schöner Steinmetzarbeit, vergoldete Spiegel und antike Stoffe erwarten die, die sich hier in das Reich der Träume begeben.*

Mimbaste, Gascony, France

Capcazal de Pachiou

Bernard Dufour

Lot, France

Artist Bernard Dufour paints a luscious picture of country life in deepest Southwestern France. He lives in a handsome 1810 house that was built on the ruins of an old mill by a well-to-do lawyer and his family. "When we acquired it in 1962, most of the interiors were original, and unchanged from the day they were completed," he recalled. "It had never been modernized, thank goodness." He purchased the house with his late wife, Martine, a noted architect. The couple set about adding a small kitchen, bathrooms, some modern amenities, but rejoiced in the radiant beauty of the mottled old plaster walls, the handsome boiseries, creaking plank floors, and romantic alcove beds. The house is surrounded by an old oak forest where vestiges of prehistoric civilizations can be found. "We stumble upon the ruins of stone huts, dolmens, stone walls, and traces of the same people who drew the magnificent images in the caves around Lascaux," related Dufour.

Previous page: In the old kitchen and dining room, a carved wall cabinet is adorned with the initials of the Dufours.
Above: In the dining room, an alcove bed is adorned with Ikat fabrics. The bed, noted Dufour, was for the use of the original family's cooks and domestic staff. The forest offers up abundant, flavorful mushrooms, including girolles and cèpes.
Right: In his office, Dufour displays photographic portraits, in progress. He uses his computer to write his monographs, and has published several books on his portraits.

Page précédente : Dans la vieille cuisine-salle à manger, un petit placard mural en bois ciselé porte les initiales des Dufour.
Ci-dessus : Dans la salle à manger, le lit d'alcôve est recouvert de tissus Ikat. C'est dans ce lit, signale Dufour, que dormaient autrefois les cuisiniers et les domestiques des propriétaires d'origine. La forêt environnante abonde de succulents champignons, dont des girolles et des cèpes.
A droite : Dans son bureau, Dufour a accroché des photos de visages, ses œuvres en cours. Il utilise son ordinateur pour rédiger ses livres et a déjà publié plusieurs ouvrages sur ses portraits.

Vorhergehende Seite: In der alten Küche, die gleichzeitig Esszimmer ist, hängt ein geschnitztes Wandschränkchen, das die Initialen der Dufours trägt.
Oben: Das Alkovenbett im Esszimmer ist mit Ikatstoffen geschmückt. Ursprünglich, so erzählt Dufour, schliefen hier die Köche und das Hauspersonal. Der Wald bietet Pilze im Überfluss, auch Pfifferlinge und Steinpilze.
Rechts: Im Arbeitszimmer hängen Porträtfotos, an denen Dufour gerade arbeitet. Am Computer schreibt er seine Bücher, er hat bereits mehrere Bildbände mit seinen Porträtfotos veröffentlicht.

Lot, France

Bernard Dufour

Right: Bernard, who previously worked in his atelier in Paris, now paints in a converted stable. The large space has beautiful light, he said.

Below: In the blue guestroom, a linen-covered bed is set into an alcove draped with a baldaquin of quilted 19th-century Toile de Jouy. Dufour noted that the walls were originally covered in handprinted wallpaper, and the pale periwinkle blue walls have taken on the textures and patina of almost two centuries. The pair of œil de bœuf windows glance light into the hallways beyond. The painting above the bed is by Bernard Dufour.

A droite : Bernard, qui travaillait autrefois dans un atelier à Paris, peint désormais dans une étable aménagée. Il est ravi de la superbe lumière qui y règne.

Ci-dessous : Dans la chambre d'amis bleue, le lit drapé de lin est enfoncé dans une alcôve et surmonté d'un baldaquin en toile de Jouy matelassée du 19e siècle. A l'origine, les murs étaient tapissés d'un papier peint imprimé à la main dont les tons pervenche ont pris près de deux siècles de textures et de patines. La paire d'œils-de-bœuf apporte de la lumière aux couloirs situés derrière. Le tableau au-dessus du lit est de Bernard Dufour.

Rechts: Früher arbeitete Bernard in einem Pariser Atelier, heute malt er in einem umgebauten Stall. Der lang gezogene Raum hat wundervolles Licht.

Unten: Der Baldachin des Alkovenbetts im blauen Gästezimmer ist mit einer gefütterten »Toile de Jouy« aus dem 19. Jahrhundert bezogen. Dufour erzählt, dass an den Wänden ursprünglich handbedruckte Tapeten angebracht waren, auf den blassen grün-blauen Wänden zeichnet sich die Struktur und Patina von fast 200 Jahren ab. Die beiden »Œil-de-bœuf«-Fenster versehen die darunter liegenden Flure mit Licht. Das Gemälde über dem Bett stammt von Bernard Dufour.

Laszlo Peterfy

Visegrád, Pest, Hungary

La demeure simple et douillette du sculpteur Laszlo Peterfy est l'incarnation même du confort, de la tradition et de la chaleur humaine. Dans ce monde, la géographie reste la même mais les frontières, les noms, les nuances et les affiliations changent souvent. Artiste accompli et philosophe, Peterfy est admiré et aimé de ses amis et collègues pour la pureté de ses sculptures. Autour de lui gravitent artistes, écrivains et architectes, formant un cercle haut en couleurs et stimulant. Voyageant dans toute la Hongrie, il crée des statues puissantes et émouvantes pour les églises et les écoles. Ses œuvres inspirées apportent un soutien moral et spirituel dans les parcs et jardins de toute l'Europe. Né en Transylvanie, Peterfy vit dans une forêt en bordure de Budapest et puise sa force dans les siens et dans son environnement naturel. Sa maison, construite au 17ᵉ siècle, est restée pratiquement inchangée. Le tapis kirghize, les poteries d'art, les broderies et les meubles rustiques anciens parlent de vérités éternelles de la vie: la famille et l'expression personnelle.

Sculptor Laszlo Peterfy's simple, cozy house paints a picture of warmth, tradition and comfort where the geography stays the same but borders, names, nuances and affiliations often change. A devoted artist and philosopher, Peterfy is admired and loved by friends and colleagues for the purity of his sculptures. His is a lively and stimulating circle of artists, writers and architects. Traveling throughout Hungary he creates powerful and touching figures for churches and schools. Deeply moving, his works offer silent succor and spiritual uplift in parks and gardens throughout Europe. Peterfy, born in Transylvania, lives in a forest outside Budapest and draws his strength from his family and the natural setting. His house, built in the 17th century, has remained essentially unchanged. The Kirgiz rug and artful pottery and embroideries and antique country furniture sculpt images of life's eternal verities – family and personal expression.

In einem Gebiet, in dem die Landschaft zwar gleich bleibt, sich aber Grenzen, Namen, Meinungen und Ansichten häufig ändern, vermittelt das schlichte Haus des Bildhauers Laszlo Peterfy den Eindruck von Wärme, Traditionsverbundenheit und Gemütlichkeit. Peterfy lebt für seine Kunst und für die Philosophie und gehört einem lebhaften und anregenden Kreis von Künstlern, Schriftstellern und Architekten an. Freunde und Kollegen bewundern die Ursprünglichkeit und Reinheit seiner Skulpturen, die in Parks und Gärten in ganz Europa stehen und den Eindruck von ruhiger, innerer Kraft und spiritueller Einsicht vermitteln. Peterfy ist meistens unterwegs und reist durch ganz Ungarn, wo man seine kraftvollen und anrührenden Werke in vielen Kirchen und Schulen findet. Er selbst schöpft Kraft aus seiner Familie und der Natur. In Transsilvanien geboren, lebt er heute in einem Wald bei Budapest in einem Haus aus dem 17. Jahrhundert, das im Wesentlichen unverändert blieb. Der kirgisische Teppich, die kunstvollen Keramiken und Stickereien sowie die alte bäuerliche Einrichtung formen das Bild der ewigen Grundwahrheiten des menschlichen Lebens: Familie und individuelle Ausdruckskraft.

First pages: Laszlo Peterfy's studio is surrounded by the woods of ancient Visegrád, about 30 miles from Budapest.
Previous pages: Sculptor Laszlo Peterfy and his son, Mihaly, on the vine-shaded terrace of their house. Outdoors becomes indoors: vine leaves are arranged in a pottery pitcher.
Above, right and facing page: Peterfy and his wife display their collection of pottery in the dining room and living room. The tiled fireplace mantel, floor planks, and wooden banquettes are all original to the 17th century house.

Premières pages: L'atelier de Laszlo Peterfy est cerné par la forêt de l'ancienne Wisigrad, à une cinquantaine de kilomètres de Budapest.
Double page précédente: le sculpteur Laszlo Peterfy et son fils, sur la terrasse ombragée de la maison. L'extérieur et l'intérieur fusionnent: un bouquet de feuilles de vigne dans une cruche en céramique.
Ci-dessus, à droite et page de droite: Peterfy et sa femme exposent leur collection de poteries dans le salon et la salle à manger. La cheminée en carreaux de faïence, le parquet et les banquettes en bois datent tous du 17ᵉ siècle, comme la maison.

Eingangsseiten: Laszlo Peterfys Atelier liegt mitten in den Wäldern des alten Visegrád, knapp 50 Kilometer von Budapest entfernt.
Vorhergehende Doppelseite: Der Bildhauer Laszlo Peterfy und sein Sohn Mihaly auf der weinumrankten Terrasse vor ihrem Haus.
Oben, rechts und rechte Seite: Peterfy und seine Frau stellen ihre Keramiksammlung im Ess- und Wohnzimmer aus. Der Kaminaufsatz aus Fayencefliesen, die Holzdielen und die Holzbank gehörten schon immer zu diesem Haus aus dem 17. Jahrhundert.

Visegrád, Pest, Hungary   Laszlo Peterfy

Above and right: The bedroom is Peterfy's elegy to traditional painted furniture from country houses in Hungary and Germany. The pottery is part of his lifelong collection of handpainted works.
Facing page: Peterfy collected the naturally shed deer and wild sheep horns in the forest and remarked that the animals were not victims of hunters. His small sculptures grace a ledge above a banquette covered in sheepskin and a handstitched pillow.

Ci-dessus et à droite: la chambre de Peterfy est une élégie aux meubles peints traditionnels des maisons de campagne hongroises et allemandes. Il collectionne depuis toujours des objets peints à la main, dont ces poteries.
Page de droite: Peterfy ramasse les bois de cerfs et les cornes de bouquetins tombés naturellement et insiste sur le fait qu'aucun de ces animaux n'a été victime de chasseurs. Ses petites sculptures ornent une corniche au-dessus d'une banquette recouverte d'une peau de mouton et d'un coussin brodé à la main.

Oben und rechts: Das Schlafzimmer ist eine Hommage an die traditionellen bemalten Möbel in ungarischen und deutschen Landhäusern. Schon als Jugendlicher begann er handbemalte Keramiken zu sammeln, von denen hier mehrere zu sehen sind.
Rechte Seite: Peterfy fand das abgestoßene Hirschgeweih und die Hörner eines wilden Schafs im Wald. Er betont, dass es sich nicht um Jagdbeute handelt. Kleine, von ihm gefertigte Figuren schmücken den Sims über der Holzbank, auf der ein Schaffell und ein handbesticktes Kissen liegen.

Richard Stadler

Near Kufstein, Tyrol, Austria

Le philosophe et ingénieur Richard Stadler rêvait d'un chalet ancien mais, ne trouvant pas la maison de ses rêves, finit par la bâtir lui-même avec des troncs vieux de quatre siècles récupérés dans des fermes de montagne en démolition. Son chalet romantique, construit il y a 28 ans, fait 75 mètres carrés et compte trois pièces et demie. Outre deux poêles traditionnels en faïence, il est équipé d'un chauffage électrique invisible pour les longues nuits d'hiver. Dans chaque coin, des poutres baroques sculptées réchauffent les esprits. Dans une petite hutte près du chalet vivent deux jeunes daims apprivoisés qui viennent manger dans la main des invités. A l'ombre des pittoresques Alpes Kitzbühel et face au massif du Kaisergebirge, le chalet de Stadler est entouré d'arbres. « L'été est généralement ensoleillé et l'air de la montagne est très relaxant» observe-t-il. «C'est si beau que je ne bouge jamais d'ici entre mai et septembre». L'hiver, il chausse ses skis. Ses amis viennent souvent le retrouver pour un week-end de ski ou de randonnée.

Philosopher and engineer Richard Stadler had wanted to buy a historic chalet, but did not find his dream cottage, so he created it with 400-year-old timbers from demolished hillside farmhouses. His romantic chalet, which he crafted 28 years ago, has three and a half rooms, and measures 800 square feet. It has two traditional tiled stoves and concealed electric heating for winter nights, and in each corner, bold timbers with baroque carvings warm the spirit. Near the chalet, in a small hut, live two young deer which are so friendly they venture up to the chalet and eat out of guests' hands. In the shadow of the dramatic Kitzbühel Alps and facing the grand Kaiser mountain, Stadler's chalet is surrounded by trees. "In summer the weather is usually sunny and the mountain air is very relaxing," Richard Stadler noted. "I never travel from May until September because it so beautiful here." In winter, he skis. Friends often visit for a weekend of hiking or skiing.

Der Philosoph und Ingenieur Richard Stadler wollte eigentlich ein historisches Chalet kaufen, konnte aber sein Traumhäuschen nicht finden. Deshalb schuf er es selbst aus 400 Jahre alten Holzbalken, die von abgerissenen Berghöfen stammten. Sein romantisches Chalet, das er vor 28 Jahren errichtete, verfügt über dreieinhalb Zimmer und eine Wohnfläche von 75 Quadratmetern. Zwei traditionelle gefliste Öfen und die versteckte elektrische Heizung halten es in Winternächten warm, während in jeder Ecke kühne Holzbalken mit barocken Schnitzereien das Auge erfreuen. Nebenan wohnen in einer kleinen Hütte zwei junge Rehe, die so zahm sind, dass sie sogar vorbeikommen und den Gästen aus der Hand fressen. Das Chalet liegt umgeben von Bäumen im Schatten der dramatischen Kitzbüheler Alpen und mit Blick auf das Kaisergebirge. »Im Sommer ist es hier meistens sonnig und die Bergluft entspannt sehr«, erzählt Richard Stadler. »Zwischen Mai und September verreise ich nie, weil es hier so schön ist.« Im Winter fährt er Ski und am Wochenende kommen oft Freunde vorbei, um zu wandern oder Ski zu fahren.

Sabine Oberholzer and Renato Tagli

Cevio, Ticino, Switzerland

Graphistes et cyber-artistes, Renato Tagli et Sabine Oberholzer habitent dans le petit village de Cevio, dans la région ensoleillée de Ticino, à portée d'iodlé de la frontière italienne. L'esprit alerte et créatif de Renato faisant des merveilles dans le monde de la technologie, de l'informatique et de l'Internet, on peut s'étonner que sa curiosité s'applique avec le même bonheur et des résultats aussi magiques aux arbres et aux paysages. Il y a quinze ans, il a commencé à travailler avec les rythmes lents de la nature dans le jardin de leur maison, une bâtisse du 17ᵉ siècle. Nouant des pierres, des branches et des brindilles, il crée des courbes et des volutes, des arcs et des boucles. Dans les pièces de leur vieille maison de famille où règne une atmosphère de chapelle, Renato Tagli a peint de grandes toiles graphiques avec des gestes évoquant les lignes souples de ses branches qui épousent les formes des pierres. Les mobiles qui tournoient au plafond rappellent les caprices abstraits et inattendus d'une nature vénérée et remodelée.

Graphic designers and web artists Renato Tagli and Sabine Oberholzer live in the small village of Cevio in sunny Ticino within yodeling distance of the Italian border. Renato's lively creative mind has been applied most successfully and enthusiastically to the world of technology, computers and the internet, so it is perhaps surprising that his curiosity would also be applied with quirky and magical results to trees and landscapes. Fifteen years ago, he began working with the slow rhythms of nature in the garden of their house dating from the 17th century. Tying stones, knots and twigs, he creates curves and twists, arcs and loops. In the chapel-like interiors of the old family house, Renato Tagli has painted large, graphic canvases with gestures that suggest the wild bends of his stone-shaped branches. Mobiles whirling in the ceiling recall the abstract and unexpected turns of nature adored and reshaped.

Die Grafiker und Web-Künstler Renato Tagli und Sabine Oberholzer leben in dem kleinen Dorf Cevio im sonnigen Tessin, in Rufweite der italienischen Grenze. Der temperamentvolle Renato beschäftigt sich begeistert und erfolgreich mit der Welt der Technik, mit Computern und dem Internet. Daher ist man zunächst erstaunt darüber, dass er sich auch für Bäume und Landschaft interessiert und skurrile und magisch anmutende Objekte gestaltet. Vor 15 Jahren begann Renato Tagli, den langsamen Rhythmus der Natur aufgreifend, im Garten ihres Hauses zu arbeiten, das aus dem 17. Jahrhundert stammt. Er verband Steine, Knoten und Zweige zu spiralförmig gebogenen Gebilden, Schleifen und Schlingen. Im kapellenartigen Inneren des alten Hauses hängen seine großformatigen Gemälde mit Darstellungen, die den fantastischen Windungen seiner aus Steinen und Zweigen geschaffenen Objekte nachempfunden sind. An der Decke kreisende Mobiles erinnern an die abstrakten und unerwarteten Wendungen einer vom Menschen bewunderten und neu geformten Natur.

First and previous pages: Manipulating branches, shoots and limbs with stones, ties, wreaths and abstract weaving techniques Tagli turns trees into airy scribbles and land art. Nature, carefully protected within 350-year-old stone walls, happily joins along in his playful art.
Right and below: Renato Tagli, known as Cick, and Sabine Oberholzer, with one eye on the internet, another on icons of mid-century design, live with classics by Le Corbusier, Ray and Charles Eames, and Harry Bertoia.

Premières pages et double page précédente: Manipulant des branches et de jeunes pousses à l'aide de pierres, de liens, de tressages et de techniques de tissage abstraites, Tagli transforme les arbres en griffonnages aériens et il pratique l'art du paysage. La nature, soigneusement protégée derrière les murs de pierre vieux de 350 ans, se prête volontiers à ces jeux artistiques.
A droite et ci-dessous: Renato Tagli, surnommé Cick, et Sabine Oberholzer, ont un œil rivé sur Internet et l'autre sur les grands designers du milieu du 20ᵉ siècle. Ils cohabitent avec des classiques de Le Corbusier, de Ray et Charles Eames et d'Harry Bertoia.

Einganggseiten und vorhergehende Doppelseite: In einer abstrakten Flechttechnik dreht, knotet, schlingt und verknüpft Tagli Zweige, junge Triebe und Äste mit Steinen und lässt aus Bäumen luftige »Land-Art«-Gebilde entstehen. Der Garten, sorgfältig hinter 350 Jahre alten Steinmauern geschützt, und diese spielerische Kunstform gehen miteinander eine heitere Verbindung ein.
Rechts und unten: Renato Tagli, den alle Cick nennen, und Sabine Oberholzer verbinden die Welt des Internets mit Ikonen des klassischen Designs und leben mit Klassikern von Le Corbusier, Ray und Charles Eames sowie Harry Bertoia.

Above: Renato and Sabine love to take meals in the kitchen which has kept its original huge fireplace, and the blue painted ancient stone sink which serves today as storage unit.
Right: The rice paper lamp was designed by Renato Tagli. The Eames chair stands on the original stone floor. The door leads to the artist's studio.

Ci-dessus: Renato et Sabine adorent prendre leur repas dans la cuisine qui a conservé son immense cheminée d'origine et son ancien évier en pierre peint en bleu, désormais converti en niche de rangement.
A droite: La lampe en papier de riz a été dessinée par Renato Tagli. Sur le sol dallé d'origine, une chaise de Charles et Ray Eames. La porte donne sur l'atelier de l'artiste.

Oben: Am liebsten essen Renato und Sabine in der Küche, in der noch der riesige originale Kamin und die blau gestrichene Spüle stehen – letztere dient heute als Vorratsnische.
Rechts: Die Lampe aus Reispapier ist ein Entwurf von Renato Tagli, die Eames-Stühle stehen auf dem Originalsteinfußboden. Die Tür führt zum Atelier des Künstlers.

Katrin Arens

Pontida, Lombardy, Italy

L'écologie, ce concept fourre-tout optimiste et souvent vaporeux des amoureux de la planète, se métamorphose en mode de vie essentiel, concentré et fervent à la campagne. Les arbres, les pierres, la pureté de l'air et de l'eau ainsi que tous les aspects de la vie quotidienne revêtent une qualité spirituelle urgente. Protéger et soigner les forêts et les flancs de collines devient une philosophie de travail, une vraie vocation. On passe ses après-midi dans les prés printaniers pour mieux humer l'odeur des jeunes pousses tendres et sentir la terre se réchauffer sous un ciel lapis-lazuli. La logique et l'émotion ne peuvent tolérer qu'un arbre soit abattu ou qu'une famille d'oiseaux soit délogée sans de bonnes raisons. Une rangée de peupliers droits et effilés bordant un ruisseau regorgeant de cresson nécessite beaucoup de soins et d'attention. C'est pourquoi l'artiste et designer allemande Katrin Arens travaille avec un sens très affûté de l'écologie dans son moulin du 15ᵉ siècle à Pontida, près de Bergame, au pied des Alpes italiennes.

Ecology, that optimistic, often woozy catch-all concept of planet-lovers everywhere, metamorphoses into a fervent, focused, essential way of life in the countryside. Trees, stones, the purity of the air and water and every aspect of daily life take on an urgent spiritual quality. Protecting and nurturing forests and hillsides become a working philosophy, felt deep in the heart. Afternoons may be spent lolling in spring meadows the better to smell tender new shoots and feel the warming earth beneath a lapis lazuli sky. Logic and emotion can never allow a tree to be chopped carelessly or a bird-haven to be uprooted. A row of old poplar trees, straight and slender along a watercress-clogged stream, require care and attention. So German artist-designer Katrin Arens works with a fine-tuned sense of ecology in a 15th-century mill in Pontida near Bergamo, on the foothill of the Italian Alps.

Ökologie – dieser optimistische, oft vage verwendete Sammelbegriff eines bestimmten Lebenskonzepts von Naturliebhabern auf der ganzen Welt – wird, wenn man selbst auf dem Land lebt, zu einer essenziellen, klar fokussierten und leidenschaftlich vertretenen Lebensform. Bäume, Steine, Reinheit von Luft und Wasser, jeder Aspekt des täglichen Lebens bekommt eine unmittelbare spirituelle Qualität. Der Schutz von Wäldern und Berglandschaften wird zu einer im tiefsten Inneren verspürten Lebensphilosophie. Die Nachmittage verbringt man faul im Gras der Frühjahrswiesen, atmet den Duft der zarten jungen Schösslinge ein und spürt unter sich die wärmende Erde, überwölbt von einem lapislazuliblauen Himmel. Vernunft und Gefühl verbieten, grundlos einen Baum abzusägen oder ein Vogelnest zu zerstören. Eine Allee alter Pappeln, die gerade und aufrecht neben einem mit Brunnenkresse bewachsenen Bachlauf stehen, braucht Pflege und Aufmerksamkeit. Die deutsche Künstlerin und Designerin Katrin Arens arbeitet mit ausgeprägtem Sinn für Ökologie in einer Mühle aus dem 15. Jahrhundert in Pontida, nahe bei Bergamo an den Ausläufern der italienischen Alpen.

Previous pages: Beneath the vaulted ceiling Katrin Arens composed sweet harmony with white walls, a Sri Lankan caned bench, and a handcrafted table on a black slate floor.
Facing page and right: A Guatemalan fish and "Tradewinds" cabinets composed her hymn to the beauty of the natural world. Poetry in wood: a bed by Katrin Arens called "I dreamed of you".
Above: *Old salvaged timbers from demolished houses were pressed into service as a graphic plate-holder for Majorcan pottery.*

Double page précédente: *Sous le plafond voûté, Katrin a créé une douce harmonie entre des murs blancs, un banc cannelé rapporté du Sri Lanka et une table artisanale posée sur un sol en dalles d'ardoises.*
Page de gauche et à droite: *Un poisson guatémaltèque et une armoire «alizés» composent un hymne à la beauté du monde naturel. La poésie du bois: un lit de Katrin Arens baptisé «J'ai rêvé de toi».*
Ci-dessus: *De vieilles planches récupérées dans des bâtisses en démolition ont retrouvé une nouvelle vie sous forme de vaisselier aux lignes géométriques présentant des poteries de Majorque.*

Vorhergehende Doppelseite: *Unter der gewölbtem Decke verschmelzen die Bambus-Bank aus Sri Lanka, der handgearbeitete Tisch auf dem schwarzen Schieferfußboden und die weiß gestrichenen Wände zu einem harmonischen Ensemble.*
Linke Seite und rechts: *Ein Fisch aus Guatemala und die »Passat«-Schränke bilden eine Hymne an die Schönheit der Natur. Poesie in Holz: Ein Bett von Katrin Arens mit dem Namen »Ich träumte von dir«.*
Oben: *Aus dem alten Bauholz abgerissener Häuser fertigte Katrin Arens einen Schrank für ihre mallorquinischen Töpferwaren.*

Monica Sangberg Moen and Stefano Crivelli

Barberino di Mugello, Tuscany, Italy

Il y a dix ans, l'artiste suédoise Monica Sangberg Moen et l'architecte italo-américain Stefano Crivelli exploraient la campagne toscane une soixantaine de kilomètres au nord de Florence lorsqu'ils tombèrent en arrêt devant un portail en fer. «Je l'ai tout de suite reconnue» explique Monica. «C'était ma maison, elle m'attendait. Pour y accéder, il fallait ramper sous des fils de fer barbelé et des ronces chargées de mûres». En fait, il s'agissait de deux maisons de famille, l'une datant du 13ᵉ siècle, l'autre du 16ᵉ siècle, qui avaient été réunies en un seul bâtiment. A l'intérieur, il n'y avait pas grand chose à voir hormis une cheminée noircie et deux vieilles motocyclettes. Aujourd'hui, elle est meublée d'antiquités qui se sont adaptées aux différentes pièces comme les éléments d'un puzzle. «Comme toute vieille maison, la nôtre à son âme», confie Monica. «Elle est particulièrement douce et apaisante. Tout ici est un peu éphémère, un peu sérieux, un peu ludique... comme la vie».

About ten years ago, Monica Sangberg Moen and Stefano Crivelli were out exploring forty miles north of Florence when they fell into a kind of trance. Artist Monica, who is Swedish, and architect Stefano, who is Italian-American, came upon an old iron gate. "I recognized it right away," recalled Monica. "It was my house, and it was waiting for me. To get to it, we had to crawl through barbed wire and thorned blackberry bushes." It was actually two family houses, one from the 13th-century and the other from the 16th-century, which were joined and turned into one house. Inside there was little to see but a blackened fireplace and a couple of old motorcycles. Now it is furnished with antiques that adapted to the rooms like pieces of a puzzle. "As with any old house, ours has its own individual soul," said Monica. "Its spirit is particularly kind and comforting. Everything here is a little temporary, a little serious, and a little playful, just like life."

Vor etwa zehn Jahren entdeckten Monica Sangberg Moen und Stefano Crivelli bei einem Ausflug dieses Haus ungefähr 60 Kilometer nördlich von Florenz und verliebten sich auf Anhieb. Die schwedische Künstlerin Monica und der italienisch-amerikanische Architekt Stefano standen damals vor dem alten Eisentor: »Ich wusste es sofort«, erinnert sich Monica. »Hier stand mein Haus und es wartete auf mich. Um hineinzukommen, mussten wir durch Stacheldraht und torniges Brombeergestrüpp kriechen.« Eigentlich waren es zwei Gebäude, eines aus dem 13. Jahrhundert und das andere aus dem 16. Jahrhundert, die man zusammengelegt hatte. Im Inneren gab es nicht viel zu sehen außer einem verrußten Kamin und ein paar alten Motorrädern. Jetzt ist das Haus mit Antiquitäten eingerichtet, die gut in die Räume passen. »So wie jedes alte Haus hat auch dieses eine eigene Seele«, meint Monica. »Und unser Haus ist besonders freundlich und angenehm. Alles hier ist ein bisschen provisorisch, ein bisschen ernsthaft und ein bisschen verspielt – eben so wie das Leben.«

Previous pages: The old farmhouse rescued by Monica Sangberg Moen and Stefano Crivelli stands squarely on the hilltop overlooking undulating hills, with no signs of people. The house and the wood-shed were built of stone from local quarries. That's country life: dreaming beside the mulberry tree in the golden light of afternoon.
Facing page: the entry gate. It was exactly this mysterious, halfdeserted landscape that first drew Monica and Stefano to their domain.
Above: an impromptu lunch served on a hand-hewn table near the mulberry tree.

Double page précédente: La vieille ferme sauvée par Monica Sangberg Moen et Stefano Crivelli se dresse fièrement au sommet d'une colline, surplombant un paysage vallonné. Aucune autre habitation n'est visible à la ronde. La maison et sa remise ont été construites avec des pierres extraites de carrières locales. Country Life: rêver sous son mûrier dans la lumière dorée de l'après-midi.
Page de gauche: le portail d'entrée. C'est ce paysage mystérieux et à demi abandonné qui a attiré Monica et Stefano.
Ci-dessus: un déjeuner improvisé servi sous le mûrier.

Vorhergehende Doppelseite: Unerschütterlich steht das alte, von Monica Sangberg Moen und Stefano Crivelli restaurierte Landhaus auf dem kleinen Berg. Von hier aus hat man einen herrlichen Blick auf die hügelige menschenleere Landschaft. Die Steine für das Haus und den Holzschuppen kommen aus nahe gelegenen Steinbrüchen. Das ist Landleben: unter einem stattlichen alten Maulbeerbaum im goldenen Licht der Nachmittagssonne Träumereien nachhängen.
Linke Seite: das Gartentor. Es war genau diese geheimnisvolle, halb-verlassene Atmosphäre, die Monica und Stefano von Anfang an in ihren Bann zog.
Oben: ein improvisiertes Mittagessen auf einem selbstgezimmerten Tisch neben dem Maulbeerbaum.

Below and facing page: The transitional rooms of the house have been handled with great bravado, warmed with Turkish rugs, framed in bold brick doorways, and graced with a simple staircase.

Ci-dessous et page de droite: Les pièces de passage de la maison ont été traitées avec panache, réchauffées par des tapis turcs. Le pourtour des portes a été laissé en briques nues. L'escalier a la grâce de la simplicité.

Unten und rechte Seite: Die kühn gestalteten Durchgangsräume wirken durch den türkischen Teppich, die Torbögen aus Ziegelsteinen und das schlichte Treppenhaus einladend.

Above: There is always a push-and-pull when refurbishing and restoring a 500-year-old house. The couple worked with great respect and devotion, still bestowing on it the blessings of today's aesthetic. Monica and Stefano danced this waltz together, and orchestrated a balanced harmony. The old stones, bricks, beams and apertures are there – and there is the shock of the painterly green.

Ci-dessus: Restaurer et réaménager une maison vieille de cinq siècles n'est pas une mince affaire. Monica et Stefano ont abordé ensemble ce délicat pas de deux avec grand respect et dévotion, tout en apportant leur propre touche d'esthétique contemporaine. Ils ont orchestré une harmonie équilibrée: les vieilles pierres, briques, poutres et ouvertures sont toujours à leur place, rehaussées d'un vert pictural.

Oben: Ein 500 Jahre altes Haus zu restaurieren ist ein ständiges Auf und Ab. Monica und Stefano widmeten sich dieser Aufgabe mit Hingabe und Respekt, wollten aber auf eine moderne Ästhetik nicht verzichten. So schufen sie gemeinsam ein perfekt aufeinander abgestimmtes Ganzes: Sie beließen die alten Steine, Ziegel, Balken und Durchgänge und inszenierten dazu schreiend grün gestrichene Wände.

Above: Monica painted the floor and the walls of the sitting room with eco-friendly milk-based paints. Their decor includes a polyglot collection of furniture, paintings and objets trouvés.
Right: The floor of this salon is crafted from salvaged old beams.
Facing page: The wooden staircase was found discarded in a corner of the deserted villa. It fits perfectly. The old iron hand rail was a fortuitous gift to Stefano from friends.
Following pages: The couple purchase demijohns of wines, such as Chianti, and then fill their own carafes from the wicker-wrapped traditional containers. Mulberry pie is served for dessert.

Ci-dessus: Monica a enduit le sol et les murs du petit salon de peintures écologiques à base de lait. Le décor inclut une collection cosmopolite de meubles, de tableaux et d'objets trouvés.
A droite: Le sol de ce salon a été réalisé avec des poutres récupérées.
Page de droite: L'escalier en bois a été retrouvé, oublié, dans un coin de la bâtisse abandonnée. Il a trouvé sa juste place. La vieille rampe en fer est un cadeau providentiel des amis de Stefano.
Double page suivante: Le couple achète des dames-jeannes de vin, puis remplit ses carafes à partir de ces bonbonnes traditionnelles gainées d'osier. La tarte aux mûres est gardée pour le dessert.

Oben: Monica versah den Boden und die Wände im Wohnzimmer mit einem umweltfreundlichen Anstrich auf Milchbasis. Die Einrichtung besteht aus einer bunten Sammlung von Möbeln, Gemälden und Objekten aus aller Welt.
Rechts: Der Fußboden wurde mit wieder verwendeten Balken belegt.
Rechte Seite: Die Holztreppe lag in einer Ecke der verlassenen Villa. Den alten Handlauf aus Eisen bekam Stefano von Freunden geschenkt.
Folgende Doppelseite: Monica und Stefano kaufen Wein in großen Korbflaschen und füllen ihn dann in kleinere Flaschen um. Zum Nachtisch gibt es Maulbeerkuchen.

Barberino di Mugello, Tuscany, Italy

Monica Sangberg Moen and Stefano Crivelli

Above: Monica Sangberg Moen's studio, newly created in the villa, has the ideal light. Monica has exhibited throughout Europe, including Italy, Sweden and Switzerland.
Right: In the bedroom on the second floor, the Swedish headboard, with its ruffles and flourishes, was painted by a talented family member.
Facing page: Sangberg Moen and Crivelli understand the power of color to startle, and stimulate. "The house has great atmosphere," said the couple. "It's very calm and silent, with beautiful light."

Ci-dessus: L'atelier de Monica Sangberg Moen, récemment créé, jouit d'une lumière idéale. Monica a exposé dans toute l'Europe, y compris en Italie, en Suède et en Suisse.
A droite: Dans la chambre du premier étage, la tête de lit suédoise, avec ses arabesques et entrelacs, a été peinte par un talentueux membre de la famille.
Page de droite: Sangberg Moen et Crivelli comprennent le pouvoir de la couleur qui surprend et stimule. « La maison a une belle atmosphère », confie le couple.« Elle est très calme et silencieuse, avec une lumière superbe ».

Oben: Das Atelier von Monica Sangberg Moen wurde erst vor kurzem fertiggestellt und verfügt über idealen Lichteinfall. Monicas Werke wurden in ganz Europa ausgestellt, auch in Italien, Schweden und der Schweiz.
Rechts: Das Schlafzimmer liegt im Obergeschoss. Ein Familienmitglied bemalte das aus Schweden stammende Kopfende des Bettes mit Ornamenten und Schnörkeln.
Rechte Seite: Sangberg Moen und Crivelli wissen um die Kraft der Farben, wenn es um verblüffende oder anregende Effekte geht. »Das Haus hat sehr viel Atmosphäre«, sagen beide. »Es ist sehr ruhig und still, mit wundervollem Licht.«

Barberino di Mugello, Tuscany, Italy

Monica Sangberg Moen and Stefano Crivelli

Leisa and Michael Snyder

Near Florence, Tuscany, Italy

Leisa et Michael Snyder – elle est décoratrice, il est cadre dans une multinationale – étaient parfaitement heureux à San Francisco. Se promenant sur les falaises voisines, faisant du vélo le long de la côte, ils ne pouvaient imaginer une vie meilleure. Puis Michael fut muté à Florence et ils optèrent pour une immersion totale, culturelle et professionnelle, dans l'expérience florentine. Ils dénichèrent une ancienne ferme du 17e siècle juste en dehors de la ville et décidèrent de la transformer en maison de famille simple et douillette. «Il y avait beaucoup d'espace pour nos deux enfants, Audrey et Griffin, et des endroits pour profiter au mieux de toutes les saisons», raconte Leisa. Elle a mélangé des meubles contemporains rapportés de Californie avec des antiquités d'Italie du nord et de nouvelles pièces découvertes lors de promenades autour de Florence. La bâtisse possède également une tourelle, qui servait autrefois de tour de guet. «Elle était située en dehors des remparts de la ville» explique Michael. Ils sont entourés d'oliviers et jouissent de vues somptueuses sur les collines environnantes.

Leisa and Michael Snyder – she's an interior designer, he's an executive of a multinational company – were very happy living in San Francisco. Hiking in the nearby Headlands, biking along the bay, they could not imagine a better life. But then Michael was posted to Florence, and they decided to work, study, and have the full Florentine experience. They found a 17th-century house just outside Florence and decided to turn it into a cozy, simple family house. "There was lots of space for our two children, Audrey and Griffin, and places to enjoy the best of the seasons," said Leisa. She mixed contemporary furniture from California with antiques from Northern Italy, and new pieces found in their wandering around Florence. Originally a working farmhouse, their house has a turret, once used as a watchtower. "It's outside the protection of the walls of the city," explained Michael. They're surrounded by an olive grove and have wonderful views of surrounding hills.

Leisa Synder ist Interior-Designerin und ihr Mann Michael arbeitet in einem internationalen Unternehmen. Sie lebten früher sehr glücklich in San Francisco, wanderten dort in den nahe gelegenen Headlands, radelten an der Küste entlang und konnten sich kein besseres Leben vorstellen. Aber als Michael dann nach Florenz versetzt wurde, beschlossen sie, sich beruflich und auch privat ganz auf das florentinische Lebensgefühl einzulassen. Sie fanden ein Haus aus dem 17. Jahrhundert in den Hügeln außerhalb von Florenz und verwandelten es in ein gemütliches, einfaches Heim für ihre Familie. »Hier gibt es jede Menge Platz für unsere beiden Kinder, Audrey und Griffin, und man kann hier alle Jahreszeiten genießen«, erzählt Leisa. In den Räumen mischte sie moderne kalifornische Designmöbel und Antiquitäten aus Norditalien mit neuen Objekten, die sie bei Streifzügen durch Florenz entdeckt. Das Gebäude war ursprünglich ein Bauernhaus und verfügt über einen kleinen Turm, der früher als Wachturm diente. »Denn das Haus steht gerade außerhalb der Schutzmauern der Stadt«, erklärt Michael. Es ist von Olivenbäumen umgeben und man hat von hier aus einen herrlichen Blick auf die umliegenden Hügel.

Below: The ceramic heart box and candleholder on the old dresser were made by Griffin and Audrey as gifts for their mother.
Facing page: In the living room, Leisa designed an overscale ottoman. It's calfskin printed with a zebra motif.
Following pages: The bed is draped with a golden cotton damask bedspread. On an old brass shelf in the bathroom, the Snyders arranged a collection of artisan soaps, and floral scented oils. Indoors: Murano glass, dahlias, orchids and bougainvillea. Outdoors: Griffin plays soccer with his mother, and the table is set with Nambé plates.

Ci-dessous: La boîte en forme de cœur et le bougeoir en céramique sur la vieille coiffeuse sont des cadeaux confectionnés par Audrey et Griffin pour leur mère.
Page de droite: Pour la salle de séjour, Leisa a dessiné une banquette géante, tapissée de veau imprimé façon zèbre.
Double page suivante: Le lit est drapé d'un damassé en coton doré. Dans la salle de bains, sur une vieille étagère en cuivre, les Snyder ont disposé un assortiment de savons et d'huiles parfumés. A l'intérieur, des verreries de Murano, des dahlias, des orchidées et des bougainvilliers. Au-dehors, Griffin joue au football avec sa mère tandis que la table est dressée avec des assiettes Nambé.

Unten: Die herzförmige Keramikdose und den Kerzenständer bastelten Griffin und Audrey als Geschenk für ihre Mutter.
Rechte Seite: Für das Wohnzimmer designte Leisa einen riesigen, mit Kalbsfell bezogenen Hocker mit aufgedrucktem Zebramuster.
Folgende Doppelseiten: Als Bettüberwurf dient eine Tagesdecke aus goldfarbenem Baumwolldamast. Auf einem alten Messingregal im Bad stehen kleine handgemachte Seifen. Im Haus: Muranoglas, Dahlien, Orchideen und Bougainvillea. Draußen: Griffin spielt mit seiner Mutter Fußball; der Tisch ist mit Nambé-Geschirr gedeckt.

Previous pages: The noble old stone farmhouse stands like a sentinel on the crest of a hill. Cool, open spaces embrace the family who spend summer days outdoors. Daughter Audrey enjoys sunshine on the loggia. Sunlight spills into the dining room, which has a terracotta tile floor. The table, draped in white and gold silk, is surrounded by chairs slip-covered in natural linen. The chandelier is from Murano.
Above: The old stone stairway leading from the entrance to the upstairs bedroom is exactly as it was 300 years ago – with a fresh coat of white paint on the walls.

Doubles pages précédentes: La vieille et noble ferme en pierre se dresse telle une sentinelle sur la crête d'une colline. La famille passe tout l'été dehors, dans les nombreux espaces dégagés et frais. Audrey aime prendre le soleil sur la loggia. Le soleil inonde les tomettes de la salle à manger. La table, drapée d'une soie blanche et or, est entourée de chaises recouvertes de housses en lin naturel. Le lustre vient de Murano.
Ci-dessus: Le vieil escalier en pierre qui mène de l'entrée à la chambre située à l'étage est exactement tel qu'il était il y a trois siècles. Les murs, eux, ont reçu une nouvelle couche de peinture blanche.

Vorhergehende Doppelseiten: Das stattliche alte Bauernhaus aus Stein steht wie ein Wachposten auf der Hügelkuppe. Die Sommertage verbringt die Familie im Freien. Tochter Audrey genießt die Sonne auf der Loggia. Helles Licht fällt in das Esszimmer, dessen Boden mit Terrakottafliesen ausgelegt ist. Den Tisch bedeckt ein weißes und goldfarbenes Seidentuch, die Stühle sind mit Hussen aus naturfarbenem Leinen bezogen. Der Lüster stammt aus Murano.
Oben: Das Steintreppenhaus, das nach oben zu den Schlafzimmern führt, ist noch genauso wie vor 300 Jahren – nur mit einem frischen, weißen Anstrich.

Jacqueline Morabito

La Colle-sur-Loup, Côte d'Azur, France

Jacqueline Morabito est une touche-à-tout énergique. Elle a conçu des intérieurs résidentiels et commerciaux, a dessiné des bijoux en or, et est une sculptrice, styliste, designer et décoratrice en vue et très demandée. Compte tenu du rythme frénétique de ses journées intenses et visuellement stimulantes, il n'est pas étonnant que, pour son propre intérieur, elle ait opté pour la plus grande simplicité. Avec son mari, ils ont restauré une ferme abandonnée dans le vieux village perché de La Colle-sur-Loup. Cette région chargée d'histoire est prise dans un réseau de routes anciennes qui mènent de Nice à Grasse et d'Antibes à Saint-Paul-de-Vence. Chaque année, ce village jalousement protégé aux maisons dotées de toits en tuiles de terre cuite célèbre la saint Roch, patron des invalides, et la saint Eloi, patron des orfèvres. Avec une grande sensibilité et l'étroite collaboration de son architecte de mari, Morabito a restauré la carcasse de la bâtisse tout en dépouillant ses pièces dans un pur esprit minimaliste.

Jacqueline Morabito is a dynamic polymath. She has designed residential and commercial interiors, crafted gold jewelry, and is a noted and in-demand sculptor, stylist, furniture designer, and decorator. Perhaps it is not surprising, given the fast-paced, intense and visually stimulating nature of her day, that for her own home-base, she prefers utmost simplicity. She and her husband rescued an abandoned farmhouse in the historic hillside town of La Colle-sur-Loup. The region, where history runs deep, is caught in a net of ancient roads that lead from Nice to Grasse, and Antibes to St-Paul-de-Vence. This is the kind of fiercely protected old terracotta-roofed village that each year celebrates the feast days of Saint Roch, patron saint of invalids, and St Eloi, patron saint of goldsmiths. With great sensitivity, and in close consultation with her architect husband, Morabito renovated the outer shell but pared the interior down to pure, uncompromising minimalism.

Jacqueline Morabito ist dynamisch und vielseitig begabt. Sie gestaltet die Inneneinrichtung von Wohnungen und Gewerberäumen, entwirft Goldschmuck und ist auch eine gefragte Bildhauerin, Stylistin, Möbeldesignerin und Dekorateurin. Deshalb überrascht es nicht, dass sie nach ihrem intensiven, visuell stimulierenden und sehr aktiven Tag gerade in ihrem eigenen Haus Schlichtheit bevorzugt. Zusammen mit ihrem Mann rettete sie ein verlassenes Bauernhaus in dem alten Bergdorf La Colle-sur-Loup. Dieses alte Kulturland durchzieht ein dichtes Netz historischer Straßen, die von Nizza nach Grasse, von Antibes nach St-Paul-de-Vence führen. La Colle-sur-Loup besteht aus einer Ansammlung denkmalgeschützter Häuser mit Terrakottadächern und hier finden jedes Jahr Feste zu Ehren des Saint Roch, dem Schutzheiligen der Kranken, und des Saint Eloi, dem Patron der Goldschmiede, statt. Mit großer Sensibilität und in enger Abstimmung mit ihrem Mann, einem Architekten, renovierte Morabito das Äußere des Hauses, doch bei der Innenausstattung konzentrierte sie sich auf puren kompromisslosen Minimalismus.

First pages: *"The house is like two boxes, one inside the other," said Morabito. "There is the 16th-century farmhouse exterior, which we disturbed as little as possible, and there is the new, pure, clean, unembellished interior." The Morabito-designed oak tables and chairs in the dining room have a custom-made wax, marble powder and acrylic top. In the salon, a grand sofa slipcovered in white cotton is like a room-within-a-room simplicity itself.*
Right and below: *In the bathroom, a wall cabinet keeps everything at hand and easily concealed with the flick of the wrist. Relaxed, indeed.*

Premières pages: «La maison est comme deux boîtes encastrées l'une dans l'autre» explique Morabito. «Il y a la façade de la ferme qui date du 16e siècle et que nous avons touchée le moins possible, et le nouvel intérieur, pur, net, sans embellissements». Les tables et les chaises en chêne de la salle à manger, dessinées par Morabito, sont surmontées d'un plateau en cire, poudre de marbre et acrylique. Dans le salon, le grand canapé houssé de coton blanc est la simplicité même.
A droite et ci-dessous: Dans la salle de bains, un petit placard mural garde tout à portée de main et hors de vue. On ne peut pas faire plus relaxant.

Eingangsseiten: »Eigentlich ist das Haus wie zwei ineinandergesteckte Schachteln«, sagt Morabito. »Da ist einmal das Äußere des Bauernhauses aus dem 16. Jahrhundert, an dem wir so wenig wie möglich verändert haben, und dann das Innere, das modern, puristisch und schmucklos ist.« Die von Morabito entworfenen Eichentische und -stühle im Esszimmer haben eigens hierfür hergestellte Oberflächen aus Wachs, Marmorstaub und Acryl. Das große Sofa im Salon wirkt durch seine Schlichtheit wie ein Raum im Raum.
Rechts und unten: Im Badezimmerwandschrank steht alles Nötige griffbereit und wird mit einer Handbewegung auch wieder unsichtbar: Entspannung pur.

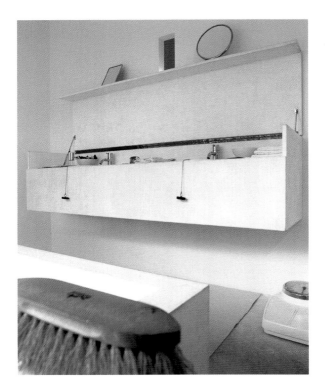

In the bedroom, Jacqueline has placed her cubic, pared-to-the-bone oak armchair, à la Donald Judd, and a bed adorned in pure white, ready for a summer siesta. Her desk chair is by the legendary French industrial designer, Jean Prouvé. True to her dictum of purity, Morabito designed walls with no moldings and resisted the temptation to add paintings or sculpture. "I like design to be very simple so that you can dream," said Jacqueline Morabito. "When you spend all day in your head, as I do, you have to live in relaxed rooms."

Dans la chambre, Jacqueline a placé son fauteuil cubique en chêne réduit à l'essentiel, à la Donald Judd, et un lit paré de blanc pur, prêt pour une sieste d'été. La chaise de son bureau est signée du légendaire dessinateur industriel Jean Prouvé. Fidèle à son goût pour la pureté, Morabito a conçu les murs sans moulures et a résisté à la tentation d'ajouter des tableaux et des sculptures. «J'aime que le design soit le plus simple que l'on puisse rêver» explique Morabito. «Quand on passe toute sa journée dans sa tête, comme c'est mon cas, il faut vivre dans des pièces relaxantes».

In Jacquelines Schlafzimmer steht ein kubischer Eichensessel à la Donald Judd, auf die reine Form reduziert. Das ganz in Weiß gehaltene Bett steht bereit für eine Sommersiesta. Der Schreibtischstuhl ist ein Entwurf des legendären französischen Industriedesigners Jean Prouvé. Jacqueline blieb ihrer Maxime treu, beließ die Wände, wie sie waren, und verzichtete auf Gemälde und Skulpuren. »Ich mag einfaches Design, in dem man schön träumen kann«, sagt Jacqueline Morabito. »Wenn man wie ich den ganzen Tag kreativ ist, sollte man in entspannten Räumen leben.«

Beryl Cavallini

Côte d'Azur, France

«Indolence» est l'un des plus beaux mots du dictionnaire. Dans le Midi de la France, c'est un art. Des transats sont disposés sous une charmille frémissante, prêts pour un pastis glacé, un papotage tranquille d'après-midi, quelques commentaires à mi-voix sur l'oranger qu'il serait peut-être temps d'arroser. On se laisse bercer par un bourdonnement d'abeilles dans un enchevêtrement de jasmin. Les battements de leurs ailes minuscules agitent des effluves fleuries, le jasmin se mêlant au parfum des fleurs d'oranger et du romarin, du basilic et de la menthe. Puis les abeilles partent butiner ailleurs. Le silence et le calme reviennent. C'est l'heure de la sieste. Les doux étés du Midi vont souvent de pair avec ces maisonnettes qu'on appelle affectueusement un «cabanon». C'est aussi le nom qu'a choisi la décoratrice Beryl Cavallini pour cette vieille bâtisse pleine de charme. Tout ce qu'il faut pour profiter du beau temps, s'amuser et se laisser aller est à portée de main: chaises longues, vieil arrosoir en tôle, oranges gorgées de soleil, intérieurs frais et même un bar improvisé pour recevoir des amis.

Indolence is one of the most beautiful words. In the South of France, it's an art. Deck chairs are arranged beneath the fluttering vines, ready for an icy pastis, a quiet afternoon chat, some murmured observations about the orange tree that will need watering. Bees are buzzing in a tangle of jasmine and the sound is so soothing. The beating of their tiny wings send eddies of jasmine fragrance into the air, to mingle with the perfumes of orange blossom and rosemary, basil and mint. The bees fly on to fresh fields. Stillness and silence again. It's time for a nap. Sweet summer in the south of France often means a little house affectionately called a "cabanon". And that's what interior designer Beryl Cavallini calls her charming summer retreat. Everything for warm-weather pleasure and fun and comfort is here at hand, from easy chairs, an old tin watering can, sun-ripe oranges, a cool interior to escape to, and a casual bar for convivial gatherings.

Trägheit ist ein wunderbares Wort. In Südfrankreich hat man sie zur Kunst erhoben. Liegestühle stehen unter grünen Weinranken bereit für einen eisgekühlten Pastis, eine entspannte Unterhaltung am Nachmittag, ein paar hingemurmelte Bemerkungen über den Orangenbaum, den man mal wieder gießen sollte. Man hört nur das einschläfernde Summen von Bienen, die in den Jasminbüschen umherschwirren. Ihre winzigen Flügel tragen Duftfetzen von Jasmin herüber, die sich mit dem Aroma von Orangenblüten und Rosmarin, Basilikum und Minze vermischen. Dann fliegen die Bienen weiter zu neuen Blüten und es kehrt wieder Stille ein. Zeit für ein Schläfchen. Diese wunderbaren Sommer in Südfrankreich sind oft verbunden mit einem kleinen, zärtlich »cabanon« genannten Landhaus. Und so nennt auch die Interior-Designerin Beryl Cavallini ihr altes, charmantes Bauernhaus, wo sie die Sommermonate verbringt. Hier gibt es alles, was man für Sommerspaß, Urlaub und Gemütlichkeit braucht: leichte Gartenstühle, eine alte Zinngießkanne, sonnengereifte Orangen, kühle Innenräume, die Schutz vor der gleißenden Sonne bieten, und eine Bar für einen entspannten Drink mit Freunden.

First pages: In summer, life revolves around the vine-shaded terrace, the garden, and attending to the trees. Perhaps there are some oranges to pick?
Previous pages: Beryl created the colored patterns in the new concrete floor. They're random, like a dream, and perfect for this dolce far niente cottage.
Above, right and facing page: Hot colors enliven the small kitchen and bar, where rose-colored walls and a yellow ceiling frame a painting by Walasse Ting.

Première page: L'été, la vie évolue autour de la terrasse ombragée, le jardin et les arbres. Peut-être y a-t-il quelques oranges à cueillir?
Double page précédente: Beryl a créé les motifs de couleur du nouveau sol en ciment. Ils sont aléatoires, comme dans un rêve, et parfaits pour cet antre du dolce farniente.
Ci-dessus, à droite et page de droite: Les couleurs torrides mettent de l'animation dans la petite cuisine-bar, dont les murs roses et le plafond jaune forment un cadre au tableau de Walasse Ting.

Eingangsseiten: Im Sommer spielt sich das Leben auf der weinumrankten, schattigen Terrasse oder im Garten unter den Bäumen ab.
Vorhergehende Doppelseite: Beryl gestaltete das Muster auf dem Betonboden selbst. Es besteht aus farbigen Steinen und passt perfekt zum »dolce far niente« von Le Cabanon.
Oben, rechts und rechte Seite: Kräftige Farben beleben die kleine Küche und die Bar, wo roséfarbene Wände und die gelbe Decke den idealen Rahmen für ein Gemälde von Walasse Ting bilden.

Jeanne and Jean-Marie Maréchal

Provence, France

Tous les jeunes enfants nourrissent le rêve éternel et romantique de s'enfuir avec les romanichels. C'est une fuite mythologique loin des conventions et des restrictions, vers une vie imaginaire de vagabondage sans soucis. Les Tziganes, venus à l'origine du nord de l'Inde et nomades par choix, sillonnent l'Europe, l'Angleterre et l'Irlande depuis le 11e siècle. Au début du 19e siècle, ils se mirent à voyager de ville en ville dans des carrioles peintes et ouvragées. Aujourd'hui, ces dernières ont été supplantées par les véhicules modernes mais il en subsiste encore quelques-unes. En Provence, Jeanne et Jean-Marie Maréchal sont tombés sous le charme de ces roulottes traditionnelles et ont fait de la sauvegarde et de la restauration de ces reliques culturelles leur mission. De nombreuses caravanes sont tombées en poussière avec le temps, alors que d'autres ont été rituellement brûlées à la mort d'un patriarche. Les Maréchal ont repeint les vieilles roulottes avec leurs couleurs vives et leur iconographie allégorique traditionnelles.

Every young child entertains the eternal and romantic dream of running away with the Gypsies. It's a mythological flight from convention and restrictions, to a fantasy of life-without-care on the open road. Gypsies (Roma), originally from Northwest India and itinerant by choice, have roamed Europe, England and Ireland since the 11th century. In the early 19th century, they began to travel from town to town in painted wagons. Few of these ornate wagons are still in existence today, superceded by modern vehicles. In Provence, Jeanne and Jean-Marie Maréchal fell in love with traditional folkloric gypsy wagons ("les roulottes" in French) and have made rescuing and restoring these cultural relics a mission and their life's work. Jeanne noted that many caravans have simply been destroyed over time, while others were ritually burned upon the death of a Roma patriarch. The Maréchals repaint the old wagons with vivid colors and allegorical imagery.

Jedes Kind träumt den ewigen und romantischen Traum davon, mit Zigeunern auf große Fahrt zu gehen. Es ist eine Art mythologischer Flucht vor den Konventionen und Grenzen des Alltags, hin zu einem Leben auf der Straße, ohne Sorgen und Zwänge. Die Roma stammen ursprünglich aus Nordwestindien, bereits im 11. Jahrhundert wanderten sie durch Europa. Im frühen 19. Jahrhundert begannen sie, in bunt bemalten Wagen von Stadt zu Stadt zu ziehen. Heute gibt es nur noch wenige dieser reich verzierten Wagen, die meisten wurden von modernen Fahrzeugen abgelöst. Jeanne und Jean-Marie Maréchal verliebten sich in die traditionellen Zigeunerwagen der Provence, die »roulottes« genannt werden, und machten es zu ihrer Lebensaufgabe, diese kulturellen Schätze zu retten und zu restaurieren. Viele Wohnwagen sind einfach mit der Zeit kaputtgegangen, oder, so erzählt Jeanne, wurden nach dem Tod eines Roma-Patriarchen verbrannt. Die Maréchals bemalen die alten Wohnwagen wieder mit den traditionellen allegorischen Bildern in kräftigen Farben.

Jeanne and Jean-Marie Maréchal redecorated their small green Gypsy
wagon in the spirit of Southern France to depict a life of ease and gai-
ety. Using vibrant colors like red, blue and green and vintage flowered
fabrics, they restored the wagon to its original splendor. With bravura
restoration, rare old textiles in colors of yesteryear, and a linen-decked
bed-with-a-view, the Maréchals induce a reverie of a vanished
vagabond life.

Jeanne et Jean-Marie Maréchal ont redécoré leur petite roulotte de gi-
tan verte dans l'esprit du Midi de la France, symbole d'une vie gaie et
facile. A l'aide de rouges, de bleus et de verts énergiques et de tissus anciens à fleurs, ils lui ont fait retrouver sa splendeur d'antan. Leur restauration audacieuse, qui inclut un lit avec vue et tapissé de lin, crée
une atmosphère nostalgique, évocatrice d'une vie itinérante comme il
n'en existe plus.

Leicht und heiter: Jeanne und Jean-Marie Maréchal richteten ihren
kleinen grünen Zigeunerwagen im südfranzösischen Stil ein. Sie verwendeten kräftige Farben wie Rot, Blau und Grün und gaben mit alten geblümten Stoffen dem Wagen seinen ursprünglichen Glanz
zurück. Seltene Stoffe in den Farben von einst, ein »Bett mit Aussicht« und Leinenüberwurf beschwören den Traum eines verschwun-
denen Vagabundenlebens.

Paola Pennisi

Carruba di Riposto, Sicily, Italy

Dreams and mysteries and the colorful history of a talented family seem to haunt every corner of this magical house overlooking the Gulf of Catania. Perhaps that is because the current inhabitants live within its boundaries with utmost respect and love for its poetic pink walls, old terracotta floors, and the ancient lichen-covered lava stones of its doors and mantels. Situated among orange groves and within sight of fiery Mount Etna, this is now the country house of architect Paola Pennisi, her daughter Laura, and her mother Marieluce de Vautibault. "Our residence was built in the 17th century as a villa surrounded by vineyards," recounted Pennisi. "My family acquired it around 1850, and lived in it until a large earthquake in 1908 caused serious damage." In 1940, the vineyards were pulled out, and orange groves were planted. It fell to Paola's father, Paolo, an engineer to bring the house back to life. Now Paola Pennisi continues the restoration.

Previous pages: *The original hue of the ancient pink walls was achieved with a mixture of volcanic earth, plaster, and ground shells. Terracotta tiles are original to the house. The family preferred to use heirloom furniture rather than new pieces.*
Above: *For the cool, celadon-walled guest bedroom Paola Pennisi's father designed the iron double headboard. "From this window I can see Mount Etna," said Paola. "At night we watch the glowing red rivers of molten lava."*
Facing page: *Laura plays peek-a-boo.*

Double page précédente: *La teinte originale vieux rose des murs a été obtenue en mélangeant de la terre volcanique, du plâtre et de la poudre de coquillages. Pour mettre en valeur l'harmonie rustique des pièces anciennes, rien de tel que de vieux meubles de famille.*
Ci-dessus: *Dans la chambre d'amis fraîche aux murs vert céladon, Paolo, le père de Paola Pennisi, a dessiné la double tête de lit en fer forgé. «De cette fenêtre, je peux voir l'Etna» affirme Paola. «La nuit, on voir rougeoyer les rivières de lave en fusion».*
Page de droite: *Laura joue à cache-cache.*

Vorhergehende Doppelseiten: *Um den ursprünglichen Pinkton der Wände wiederherzustellen, wurde Vulkanerde mit Mörtel und zerriebenen Muschelschalen gemischt. Die alten Terrakottafliesen wurden belassen. Die Familie richtete das Haus mit Erbstücken ein.*
Oben: *Für das in kühlen, blass-grünen Farben gehaltene Gästezimmer entwarf Paolas Vater ein Doppelbett mit einem eisernen Kopfteil. »Von diesem Fenster aus kann man den Ätna sehen«, erklärt Paola. »Nachts beobachten wir oft die rot glühenden Lavaströme.«*
Rechte Seite: *Laura spielt Verstecken.*

Facing page: The large living room required extensive restoration. Paola Pennisi, who describes the house as her ongoing project, re-designed the fireplace. It is framed with massive pieces of lava rock, gifts of Mount Etna, a constant, colorful presence in the life of the region.

Page de gauche: Le grand salon a nécessité de nombreux travaux de restauration. Paola Pennisi, qui décrit sa maison comme un chantier perpétuel, a redessiné la cheminée. Elle est en pierre de lave, cadeau du mont Etna, une présence constante et pittoresque dans la vie de la région.

Linke Seite: Das großzügige Wohnzimmer erforderte umfangreiche Renovierungsarbeiten. Paola Pennisi, die ihr Haus als nie endende Aufgabe beschreibt, entwarf die Kamineinfassung aus massivem Lavagestein vom Ätna – Zeichen der Verbundenheit mit der Region.

Above: The downstairs guest bedroom was formerly a small chapel. "All houses in this region had their own chapels in the 19th century," noted Paola. Deconsecrated, it was sensitively restored and cleaned. The painted ceiling and architectural details of the ceiling vault were discovered during the restoration. The iron headboard was designed by Paolo Pennisi.
Left: Paola's mother's French heritage shows in the rose-patterned draperies and bedcover in her upstairs bedroom. Luxuriant bougainvillea keeps the room cool on hot summer afternoons.

Ci-dessus: La chambre d'amis au rez-de-chaussée était autrefois une petite chapelle. «Au 19ᵉ siècle, toutes les maisons de la région avaient leur chapelle», explique Paola. Revenue à la vie profane, elle a été restaurée et nettoyée. Le plafond peint et les détails de la voûte ont été découverts lors de la restauration. La tête de lit en fer forgé a été dessinée par Paolo Pennisi.
A gauche: Les origines françaises de la mère de Paola se retrouvent dans les roses qui ornent les rideaux et le couvre-lit de sa chambre. Un bougainvillier garde la pièce au frais pendant les chaudes après-midi.

Oben: Das Gästezimmer im Erdgeschoss war früher eine kleine Kapelle. »Im 19. Jahrhundert hatten hier alle Häuser ihre eigene Hauskapelle«, erzählt Paola. Da die Kapelle schon lange entweiht war, wurde der Raum sorgfältig gesäubert und renoviert, dabei kamen Deckenmalereien und Reste des Gewölbes zum Vorschein. Das Bett mit dem eisernen Kopfteil ist ein Entwurf von Paolo Pennisi.
Links: Im Obergeschoss liegt das Schlafzimmer der Mutter. Die Rosenmuster auf den Vorhängen und dem Bettüberwurf verraten ihre französische Herkunft. Üppige Bougainvillea hält den Raum auch an heißen Sommernachmittagen frisch und kühl.

Karel Fonteyne

Alayor, Menorca, Spain

Il y a neuf ans, quand le photographe belge Karel Fonteyne a débarqué à Minorque, l'île rocheuse était endormie, heureuse et accueillante. Originaire d'Anvers et spécialisé dans la mode, Fonteyne a travaillé pour le «Vogue» français, «Marie Claire» et «Interview». Lassé par le monde des falbalas, il a vendu sa maison d'Anvers et s'est réfugié à Minorque en quête de paix, de simplicité, de rusticité et d'un certain rapport à la terre. «J'adore l'énergie qui se dégage de la terre, ici» confie-t-il. Il a acheté une petite ferme vieille de quatre siècles, avec son corps principal, son étable et ses dépendances, près d'Alayor, au centre de Minorque. «Nous sommes entourés de forêts de pins et de chênes, si bien qu'on se sent très à l'abri» s'émerveille-t-il. «Toutefois, la côte et les plages ne sont qu'à dix minutes». Toute la région étant protégée, aucun nouveau bâtiment ne peut venir dénaturer le paysage. «Décorer mes maisons me permet de m'exprimer artistiquement. Je me suis beaucoup amusé à faire celle-ci, c'est le principal».

Nine years ago when Belgian photographer, Karel Fonteyne, arrived on the rocky island, Menorca was sleepy, happy, and enticing. Fonteyne, originally from Antwerp, specialised in fashion. His work was published in French *Vogue, Marie Claire* and *Interview*. Disillusioned with the fashion world, Fonteyne sold his house in Antwerp and disappeared to Menorca in search of peace, simplicity, and a certain earthiness and rusticity. "I love the energy that rises from the earth here," he said. He acquired a tiny 400-year-old cottage, stables and farm buildings near Alayor in the center of Menorca. "We're surrounded by pine and oak forests, so it feels very private," he marveled. "But the coast and beaches are just ten minutes away." The whole area is protected, so no new buildings can pop up on the landscape. "The interiors of my houses are my artistic expression," Karel said. "I had a lot of fun and that's the most important thing."

Als der belgische Fotograf Karel Fonteyne vor neun Jahren nach Menorca kam, war die Insel verschlafen, glücklich und verführerisch. Fonteyne, der aus Antwerpen stammt, war Modefotograf und veröffentlichte seine Arbeiten in der französischen »Vogue«, in »Marie Claire« und »Interview«. Desillusioniert von der Modewelt verkaufte er sein Haus in Antwerpen und verschwand nach Menorca, auf der Suche nach Frieden, Erdverbundenheit und Einfachheit. »Ich liebe die Energie, die die Erde hier ausströmt«, erklärt er. Bei Alayor im Herzen der Insel kaufte er ein winziges, 400 Jahre altes Landhaus mit zugehörigen Scheunen und Geräteschuppen. »Das Haus liegt sehr zurückgezogen und ist von Pinien und Eichenwäldern umgeben. Aber die Küste und die Strände sind nur zehn Minuten entfernt.« Die gesamte Gegend steht unter Naturschutz, so dass man nicht befürchten muss, dass plötzlich Neubauten aus dem Boden schießen. »Die Innenräume zeigen meinen künstlerischen Ausdruck«, meint er, »und ich hatte eine Menge Spaß beim Einrichten, das ist schließlich das Wichtigste.«

Facing page: Lavender, figs, palms, olives, bougainvillea, and 60 fruit trees flourish in the garden. Fonteyne painted his cottage blue. "It's the only blue house on the island," he said. "Most of the houses are white. I was inspired by the sea and the sky."
Above and right: Children love to visit the house in summer, and spend most of the day whooping and diving in the pool. In the afternoon, exhilarated from island exploration and swimming, everyone gathers on the terrace for lunch.

Page de gauche: La lavande, les figuiers, les oliviers, les bougainvilliers et 60 arbres fruitiers s'épanouissent dans le jardin. Fonteyne a peint toutes les façades en bleu. «C'est la seule maison bleue de l'île» explique-t-il. «La plupart sont blanches. J'ai été inspiré par la mer et le ciel».
Ci-dessus et à droite: Les enfants adorent venir dans cette maison l'été et passent des journées entières à sauter et plonger dans la piscine. L'après-midi, revigorés par la baignade et les promenades, tout le monde se rassemble sur la terrasse pour un déjeuner tardif.

Linke Seite: Lavendel, Feigenbäume, Palmen, Olivenbäume, Bougainvillea und 60 Obstbäume wachsen in seinem Garten. Fonteyne strich sein Haus blau: »Es ist das einzige blaue Haus auf der Insel, die meisten Häuser hier sind weiß. Das Blau des Meeres und des Himmels inspirierte mich dazu.«
Oben und rechts: Kinder lieben dieses Haus, besonders im Sommer, wenn sie den ganzen Tag draußen im Pool herumtoben und schwimmen können. Nachmittags, wenn alle von Ausflügen oder vom Schwimmen müde sind, trifft man sich auf der Terrasse zum Essen.

Below: In the library, Fonteyne's lifetime collection of "found shoes" is arranged along the mantel. Photographs on the wall are by Karel Fonteyne. The photographer loves the serendipitous clash of colors and textures, and plays with visitors' design expectations for a Menorcan country house.

Facing page: Mauve walls and pink ceilings give a festive and welcoming air to the entry. Fabrics on the soft stash of pillows were collected in Morocco. Ship models, rolls of oil paintings, a skull with horns (Fonteyne wonders if it is a water buffalo) have been gleaned at flea markets around the world.

Ci-dessous: Dans la bibliothèque, les «chaussures trouvées» que Fonteyne collectionne depuis toujours sont exposées sur le manteau de cheminée. Au mur, ses photographies. Il aime les heureux contrastes de couleurs et de textures et s'amuse à déjouer les attentes de ses visiteurs en matière de maison.

Page de droite: Dans l'entrée, les murs mauves et les plafonds roses créent une atmosphère festive et accueillante. Les coussins nonchalamment empilés sont recouverts de tissus marocains. Les maquettes de bateau, les peintures à l'huile enroulées et le crâne cornu (Fonteyne se demande s'il ne s'agit pas d'un buffle d'eau) ont été glanés dans des marchés aux puces un peu partout dans le monde.

Unten: Fonteyne hat schon seit langem eine Schwäche für gefundene Schuhe, seine Sammlung ist auf dem Kaminsims in der Bibliothek ausgestellt. Die Fotografien an der Wand sind von Karel. Er liebt das scheinbar zufällige Aufeinanderprallen von Farben und Strukturen und spielt mit den Vorstellungen, die Besucher von einem typisch menorquinischem Landhaus haben.

Rechte Seite: Mauvefarbene Wände und eine pinkfarbene Decke lassen den Eingangsbereich festlich und einladend wirken. Die Stoffe der Kissen, die hier in Stapeln aufeinander liegen, stammen aus Marokko. Die Schiffsmodelle, die aufgerollten Ölgemälde und den Schädel an der Wand, vielleicht von einem Wasserbüffel, fand Fonteyne auf Trödelmärkten in der ganzen Welt.

In the "Peter Pan" room, Karel Fonteyne made an assemblage of flotsam and jetsam collected from the coastline of Menorca. Fonteyne's cluster of buildings is ten minutes by car from a favorite, deserted beach, and within easy access of rugged hikes.

Dans la chambre «Peter Pan», Karel Fonteyne a assemblé un assortiment d'objets que la mer a rejetés sur le rivage de Minorque. Sa fermette se trouve à dix minutes en voiture de sa plage déserte préférée et est située à la croisée de beaux chemins de randonnée.

Im »Peter Pan«-Zimmer befindet sich eine Assemblage von Karel Fonteyne aus Treibgut, das er am Strand sammelte. Sein Landhaus liegt nur etwa zehn Autominuten von seinem einsamen Lieblingsstrand entfernt und auch zu Wanderungen durch die zerklüftete Landschaft ist es nicht weit.

Right: Fonteyne collected most of his furniture at antiques stores and centuries-old flea markets in Belgium. The "Matisse" room has chrome yellow painted walls and a chequered floor, in honor of the painter, who also fell in love with Mediterranean light, pulsating color, and the sensual possibilities of art-filled interiors.
Below: "At first I painted the room totally black, to be dramatic and mysterious," said Karel Fonteyne. "But then I decided it would be more interesting multi-colored." He created the fuchsia-colored paint with chalk and paint pigments. The sofa was rescued from a flea market in Antwerp.

A droite: Fonteyne a déniché la plupart de ses meubles chez des antiquaires et sur de vieux marchés aux puces de Belgique. Dans le salon «Matisse», les murs jaune de chrome et le sol en damier sont un hommage au peintre, lui aussi amoureux de la lumière de la Méditerranée, des couleurs vibrantes et des possibilités sensuelles des intérieurs remplis d'art.
Ci-dessous: «J'avais commencé par peindre cette pièce en noir, pour un effet théâtral et mystérieux. Puis j'ai décidé qu'elle serait plus intéressante multicolore» explique Fonteyne. Il a créé sa peinture fuchsia avec de la craie et des pigments. Le canapé a été déniché aux Puces d'Anvers.

Rechts: Die meisten Möbel stammen von belgischen Antiquitätenläden und Flohmärkten. Das Matisse-Zimmer hat chromgelbe Wände zu Ehren des Malers, der sich wie Karel in das Licht und die pulsierenden Farben des Mittelmeers und die sinnlichen Möglichkeiten von mit Kunstwerken gestalteten Räumen verliebte.
Unten: »Zuerst strich ich den Raum vollkommen schwarz, um eine dramatische und geheimnisvolle Atmosphäre zu erzeugen«, berichtet Karel Fonteyne. »Aber dann merkte ich, dass ich mit mehreren Farben interessantere Effekte erzielen konnte.« Für den Fuchsia-Farbton der Wände mischte er Kalk mit Farbpigmenten. Das Sofa rettete er von einem Flohmarkt in Antwerpen.

Above: *A rustic table and chairs make a perfect breakfast starting point, in the "Matisse" room.*
Right: *In the "Chiquita" room – named for the label found on bananas – children find refuge from the sun.*
Following pages: *Beds, in a region where summer temperatures soar and indoor rest and reflection become a pleasant afternoon imperative, take on greater importance. Fonteyne had the capacious bed, with its dramatic turned posts, crafted by a Belgian craftsman. Multicolored hand-blown glass decanters were found in Venice.*

Ci-dessus: *Dans le salon «Matisse», la journée commence idéalement par un petit déjeuner sur la table rustique.*
A droite: *Dans le salon «Chiquita», qui doit son nom aux étiquettes que l'on trouve sur les bananes, les enfants viennent se protéger du soleil.*
Double page suivante: *Dans une région où les températures estivales grimpent en flèche et où la sieste et la méditation au frais sont des impératifs, les lits sont de première importance. Fonteyne a fait sculpter les montants de son grand lit à baldaquin par un artisan belge. Les carafes multicolores en verre soufflé viennent de Venise.*

Oben: *Frühstücken im »Matisse«-Zimmer an dem schlichten Tisch und den einfachen Stühlen ist der perfekte Start in den Tag.*
Rechts: *Die Kinder flüchten vor der Sonne in das »Chiquita«-Zimmer, das nach der Bananenmarke benannt ist.*
Folgende Doppelseite: *In einer Gegend, in der die Temperaturen im Sommer in die Höhe schnellen und am Nachmittag Ausruhen und Relaxen im Haus obligatorisch ist, haben kühle Schlafzimmer größte Bedeutung. Fonteyne ließ dieses geräumige Bett mit seinen dramatisch gedrechselten Pfosten von einem belgischen Handwerker ausführen. Die Dekantier-Karaffen aus mundgeblasenem farbigem Glas stammen aus Venedig.*

A Hideaway in the Country

Ibiza, Spain

La campagne d'Ibiza n'a rien à voir avec sa côte. Si le littoral est en-vahi par des hordes de touristes en quête de soleil, les boîtes de nuit et des boutiques, l'intérieur des terres et les petits villages ont conservé leur éloquence discrète traditionnelle et semblent habiter un autre es-pace- temps. C'est sans doute parce que l'île a toujours su s'adapter aux envahisseurs. Les Grecs, les Carthaginois, les Romains, les Van-dales, les Byzantins, les Normands et les Catalans ont tous convoité et conquis cette île stratégique. Les résidences et les fincas ont conservé leurs racines traditionnelles, et la maison de campagne typique entre-tient un équilibre harmonieux entre les valeurs classiques d'une archi-tecture fonctionnelle et le purement pittoresque. Les traits caractéris-tiques des maisons rurales d'Ibiza incluent le «porxo» (porche) autour duquel la maison est disposée, et un portique. Une antiquaire et déco-ratrice belge a découvert avec son mari ce havre de paix au centre d'Ibiza.

Countryside Ibiza is worlds apart from coastal Ibiza. While the coast has been invaded by sun-seeking hordes, discos and shops, the hinterlands and small country towns retain much of their tra-ditional quiet eloquence, and occupy another time and place. Per-haps that is because inland Ibiza has always adapted well to inva-sions. In succession, the Greeks, Carthaginians, Romans, Vandals, the Byzantine Empire, Normans and Catalans all prized and conquered this strategic island. Residences and fincas retain their traditional roots, and the typical Ibizan country house main-tains a harmonious balance between the classic values of func-tional architectural form and the purely picturesque. Characteris-tic features of Ibizan rural architecture include the "porxo" (porch) around which the house is arranged, and an open portico. A Belgian antiques dealer and interior designer and her husband have found such an escape in the middle of Ibiza.

Welten liegen zwischen dem ländlichen Ibiza und der Küste. Während die Diskotheken und Geschäfte an der Küste von Invasionen sonnen-hungriger Horden heimgesucht werden, haben das ibizenkische Hin-terland und seine kleinen Dörfer ihre traditionelle, ruhige Lebensweise bewahrt, als lebten die Menschen dort noch in einer anderen Zeit. Vielleicht liegt das daran, dass das Binnenland sich seinen Invasoren schon immer anzupassen verstand. Nacheinander kamen Griechen, Karthager, Römer, Wandalen, Byzantiner, Normannen und schließ-lich Katalanen und alle nahmen die strategisch wichtige Insel in Be-sitz. Den Wohnhäusern und Fincas sieht man ihre traditionellen Wur-zeln an. Sie zeichnen sich aus durch die harmonische Verbindung zwischen den klassischen Merkmalen funktioneller Architektur und pittoresken Elementen. Typisch für die Fincas auf Ibiza sind der »porxo«, eine Veranda, von der die Räume eines Hauses abgehen, und ein offener Portiko. Eine belgische Antiquitätenhändlerin und In-terior-Designerin fand zusammen mit ihrem Mann einen wunderba-ren Rückzugsort mitten auf Ibiza, einen Ort der Ruhe.

Previous pages and above: *This very effective country decor relates to Ibiza in the most natural way: rustic chairs, antique lanterns and galvanized watering cans, folding deck chairs beside the pool. Even in this deeply wooded setting, summer afternoons shimmer with heat. A favorite place to gather is the vine-shaded terrace.*
Right: *The crossroads of the Mediterranean are evident on the dining terrace. The family arranged a Moroccan lantern, French garden chairs, Belgian silver, rattan chairs, a noble table of Ibizan timbers.*

Double page précédente et ci-dessus: *Ce décor campagnard très efficace reflète parfaitement le côté naturel d'Ibiza: les chaises rustiques, les vieilles lanternes, l'arrosoir en tôle et les transats au bord de la piscine. Même au cœur de la forêt, les après-midi d'été sont de véritables fournaises. On se réfugie volontiers sur la terrasse ombragée.*
A droite: *La table du dîner dressée sur la terrasse montre bien qu'on se trouve à un carrefour de la Méditerranée: une lanterne marocaine, des chaises de jardin françaises, de l'argenterie belge, des fauteuils en rotin, une table noble en bois d'Ibiza.*

Vorhergehende Doppelseite und oben: *Die Einrichtung zeigt Ibiza von seiner natürlichen Seite: rustikale Stühle, antike Lampen, galvanisierte Gießkannen und Liegestühle neben dem Pool. Sogar in dieser baumreichen Gegend flimmert die Luft an Sommernachmittagen vor Hitze. Dann ist die weinbeschattete Terrasse der Lieblingsplatz der Familie.*
Rechts: *Kulturelle Vielfalt: eine Lampe aus Marokko, französische Gartenstühle, ein silbernes Kaffeeservice aus Belgien, Rattanstühle und ein schöner ibizenkischer Holztisch.*

Here, decorating looks easy: Architectural fragments enrich a window frame; controlled colors and pattern keep decor easy-on-the-eyes; furniture with character, like this folkloric chair, please the eye; windows outlined in blue offer graphic contrast.

Ici la décoration paraît facile: des fragments d'architecture anoblissent une fenêtre; les couleurs et les motifs mesurés reposent le regard; les meubles de caractère, comme ce fauteuil folklorique, ravissent la vue; les fenêtres bordées de bleu offrent des contrastes nets.

Hier sieht Dekoration leicht und spielerisch aus: Architekturelemente verzieren einen Fensterrahmen; Farben und Muster sind zurückhaltend und entspannt; gefällig sind Möbel mit eigenem Charakter wie dieser rustikale Stuhl; blau gestrichene Fensterrahmen bieten Farbkontraste.

Ibiza, Spain

A Hideaway in the Country

No-fuss design includes antique rusted lanterns arranged on a folding picnic table; fragrant garden fruit in an old Moroccan bowl; a cool spindle headboard that allows air circulation; an endless supply of simple, basic beeswax candles for evening romance.

La décoration sans chichis inclut de vieilles lanternes rouillées disposées sur une table de pique-nique pliante; des fruits du jardin dans un vieux plat marocain embaument la pièce; une tête de lit en fuseaux laisse l'air circuler; de simples chandelles en cire d'abeille pour des dîners d'amoureux.

Das Design verzichtet auf jeden Schnickschnack: alte, schon leicht angerostete Lampen auf einem Klapptischchen; duftendes Obst aus dem Garten in einer alten marokkanischen Schale; ein Bett mit gedrechseltem Kopfteil für erfrischende Siestas; zahllose schlichte Wachskerzen zaubern abends eine romantische Stimmung.

Left: Starting with the ideal canvas of plaster walls and terracotta tile floors, the decor has been enriched with a lifetime of antiques with cosmopolitan origins. A vegetable-dye kilim rug adds a graphic counterpoint to natural cotton sofa and chair slipcovers. Fresh lemons scent the air in a Provençal pottery bowl.
Above: The simple country kitchen, with its endless supply of olive oils and vinegars, spices and fresh herbs, turns out scrumptious lunches and dinners of astonishing sophistication.

A gauche: Les murs enduits au plâtre et le carrelage en terre cuite forment une toile de fond idéale pour le décor constamment enrichi d'antiquités chinées au cours d'une vie passée à parcourir le monde. Un kilim aux teintes végétales ajoute un contrepoint graphique aux housses en coton naturel du canapé et des chaises. Des citrons frais dans une coupe en poterie provençale parfument l'air.
Ci-dessus: Dans cette cuisine campagnarde dépouillée, avec ses abondantes réserves d'huiles d'olive et de vinaigre, d'épices et d'herbes aromatiques fraîches, on prépare de délicieux déjeuners et des dîners d'une sophistication inouïe.

Links: Die hell getünchten Wände und Terrakottafliesen bieten den idealen Hintergrund für die Anitquitätensammlung aus aller Welt. Ein mit Pflanzenfarben gefärbter Kelim setzt einen grafischen Kontrapunkt zu dem naturfarbenen Leinensofa und den Stühlen mit weißen Hussen. Zitronen duften in einer Tonschale aus der Provence.
Oben: In der einfach eingerichteten Landhausküche mit ihrem schier endlosen Vorrat an Olivenöl, Essig, Gewürzen und frischen Kräutern entstehen einfache, köstliche Mittagessen, aber auch raffinierte kulinarische Höhepunkte.

Whether it's a summer house or a permanent country house, decor with soul and natural grace will always make family and guests feel at home. Guests instantly warm to rooms with beautiful cool linens, tables and shelves for instant storage, and inviting chairs on which to drape swimsuits and summer dresses.

Qu'il s'agisse d'une maison de campagne ou d'une demeure principale, parents et amis se sentent toujours chez eux dans un décor aussi inspiré et pourvu d'une grâce naturelle. Les invités succombent instantanément au charme des pièces drapées de superbes lins frais, équi-pées de tables et d'étagères où ranger leurs affaires, de chaises accueillantes où jeter leur maillot de bain ou défroisser leur robe d'été.

Egal, ob es sich um ein Ferienhaus oder ein ständig bewohntes Land-haus handelt: In einer gemütlichen Einrichtung mit natürlicher Aus-strahlung fühlen sich Bewohner und Gäste wohl. Gäste schätzen das schöne kühle Leinen, Tische und praktische Regale, in denen sie ihre Sachen schnell verstauen können, oder Stühle, auf denen man gerne seine Badesachen oder ein Sommerkleid ablegt.

Ibiza, Spain

A Hideaway in the Country

Is it 1802 or 1902 or 2002? The honest simplicity of this Ibizan room make it memorable and timeless. The old bed is handcrafted with grace and charm and awaits beneath a swoop of cooling mosquito netting – just in case. Moroccan lanterns add a worldly accent.

Sommes-nous en 1802, en 1902 ou en 2002? La franche simplicité de cette chambre la rend mémorable et atemporelle. Le vieux lit artisanal a été réalisé avec grâce et charme et attend sous une cascade rafraî-

chissante de voilage blanc, au cas où il y aurait des moustiques. Des lanternes marocaines ajoutent une note cosmopolite.

1802, 1902 oder 2002? Die Schlichtheit dieses ibizenkischen Zimmers ist absolut zeitlos. Das alte, anmutige Bett ist handgefertigt und steht für alle Fällle unter dem Moskitonetz. Marokkanische Lampen geben dem Raum eine exotische Note.

Barbara Davis

Cherry Valley, Upstate New York

Le trajet entre Manhattan et la ferme de Barbara Davis, artiste et décoratrice, constitue un voyage idyllique à travers l'histoire de l'Amérique. La route vers le nord de l'État de New York traverse la spectaculaire vallée de l'Hudson, contourne le massif des Catskill, bifurque vers les monts Adirondacks puis longe le fleuve Mohawk, soit autant de terres d'anciennes tribus indiennes. Le voyage s'achève à l'ombre des érables, sur une colline qui domine Canajoharie Creek. A 13 kilomètres de la ville la plus proche, Barbara et ses enfants – Blair, Raina, Rory et la petite dernière, Honora – vivent dans leur propre jardin d'Eden, splendide et distingué. Barbara, qui décore des intérieurs et vend des antiquités et des tissus anciens, a découvert sa maison, construite en 1790, il y a quatre ans. «Les murs étaient tapissés d'une seule couche de papier peint sous laquelle se trouvait encore la peinture d'origine. La bâtisse n'avait pas subi les affronts de la modernisation. Nous avons cohabité avec la poussière et nous sommes même mis à l'aimer», plaisante Barbara. Ici, les temps modernes ne semblent pas avoir de prise.

Driving from Manhattan to upstate New York where artist and designer Barbara Davis lives in her 1790 farmhouse is an idyllic trip through American history. The itinerary meanders north through the scenic Hudson River Valley, skirts the Catskill Mountains, and finally veers around the Adirondack Mountains and along the Mohawk River, all home to early Native American tribes. The journey ends on a maple-shaded hillside above Canajoharie Creek. Eight miles from the nearest town, Barbara and her children Blair, Raina, Rory and baby Honora live in their own splendid and stylish Arcadia. Barbara, who designs interiors and sells antique furniture and vintage textiles, first discovered her house four years ago. "The walls were covered with just one layer of wallpaper and the original paint, and the house had not suffered the indignity of modernization. We lived with dust for years and started to love it," joked Barbara. Today does not intrude.

Die Fahrt von Manhattan in den Norden des Bundesstaates New York, wo die Künstlerin und Designerin Barbara Davis in einem Farmhaus von 1790 lebt, ist eine idyllische Reise durch die amerikanische Geschichte. Die Straße windet sich am schönen Hudson River Valley entlang, streift die Catskill Mountains und biegt dann ab zu den Adirondack Mountains und zum Mohawk River – alle diese Landschaften sind alte Stammesgebiete der Indianer. Der Weg endet an einem von Ahornbäumen beschatteten Berghang am Canajoharie Creek. Dreizehn Kilometer von der nächsten Stadt entfernt wohnen hier Barbara und ihre Kinder Blair, Raina, Rory und Baby Honora in ihrem eigenen wundervollen und eleganten Arkadien. Barbara, eine Interior-Designerin, die auch Antiquitäten sowie antike Stoffe verkauft, entdeckte ihr Haus vor vier Jahren. »Die Wände bedeckte nur eine einzige Schicht Tapete und Originalfarbe und das Haus war Gott sei Dank nie modernisiert worden. Wir lebten jahrelang im Staub und wir begannen sogar, das zu mögen«, lacht Barbara. Das Heute bleibt draußen.

Previous pages, right and following pages: "My house was probably
built for a former soldier and his family who received a land grant after the Revolutionary War," surmised artist Barbara Davis. It had not
been lived in for 50 years when she found it. She painted the exterior
"drab" and furnished the old porch. "I retained as much of the original house as possible," she said. She steamed off wallpaper, cleaned
off the scratch-coat plaster, and exposed 200-year-old beams.
Above: On the porch hangs an old chalkboard with a graphic by
Raina.

Double page précédente, à droite et double page suivante: «La
maison a sans doute été construite pour un ancien soldat et sa famille
à qui on a octroyé des terres après la guerre d'Indépendance» suppute
l'artiste Barbara Davis. Lorsqu'elle l'a trouvée, elle était inhabitée depuis 50 ans. Elle a peint la façade en gris et a aménagé le vieux porche.
Elle a décollé le papier peint, nettoyé les charmants enduits au plâtre
appliqués à la truelle puis mis à nu les poutres vieilles de 200 ans.
Ci-dessus: Sous le porche, un vieux tableau noir avec un dessin de
Raina.

Vorhergehende Doppelseite, rechts und folgende Doppelseite:
»Mein Haus wurde wahrscheinlich für einen ehemaligen Soldaten
und seine Familie errichtet, die nach dem Unabhängigkeitskrieg Land
erhalten hatten«, vermutet die Künstlerin Barbara Davis. Das Gebäude war seit 50 Jahren unbewohnt, als sie es entdeckte. Sie malte
die Außenwände grau an und richtete die alte Veranda ein. »Ich erhielt so viel wie möglich von dem alten Haus «, sagt Barbara. Sie
entfernte die Tapete, reinigte die Grundierung und legte 200-jährige
Balken frei.
Oben: Auf der Veranda hängt eine alte Kreidetafel mit einer Zeich-
nung von Raina.

In the dining room, the family gathers around an old teak table. Barbara crafted the chandelier from wire fragments, and added lavish crystals. "I prefer pieces with character," she noted. In the bathroom, she and her children created a wall collage of broken mirrors, antique silver pieces and salvaged wood.

Dans la salle à manger, une vieille table en teck. Barbara a réalisé le lustre à partir de fragments de métal et y a ajouté d'opulentes pendeloques en cristal. «Je préfère les meubles qui ont du caractère» ob-

serve-t-elle. Dans la salle de bains, ses enfants et elle ont réalisé un collage de miroirs brisés, d'anciens éléments en argent et de bois de récupération.

Im Esszimmer versammelt sich die Familie an einem alten Teaktisch. Barbara fertigte den Leuchter aus Drahtstücken und ergänzte elegante Glaskristalle. »Ich bevorzuge Stücke mit Charakter«, erzählt sie. Im Badezimmer schufen Barbara und ihre Kinder eine Wandcollage aus Spiegelscherben, antiken Silberteilen und Fundholz.

Cherry Valley, Upstate New York

Barbara Davis

Barbara stenciled the green and gray walls of her bedroom with white oil paints. She prefers to use vintage fabrics, like the 1920s striped ticking, and rejoices in French silk pillows. Her next project: fixing up the 1820 farmhands' quarters at the back of her house: "It's really charming and untouched, so the work is a bit daunting."

Barbara a peint au pochoir les murs verts et gris de sa chambre avec de la peinture à l'huile blanche. Elle a un faible pour les tissus anciens, comme la toile à matelas rayée des années 1920, et adore ses oreillers recouverts de soie française. Son prochain projet: retaper les quartiers des ouvriers agricoles à l'arrière de la maison: « Il y a du pain sur la planche car ils sont vraiment charmants et intacts. »

Barbara verzierte die grüngrauen Wände ihres Schlafzimmers mit Schablonenzeichnungen in weißer Ölfarbe. Sie bevorzugt antike Stoffe wie den gestreiften Matratzendrell aus den 1920er-Jahren und sie liebt französische Seidenkissen. Ihr nächstes Projekt: die Wohnräume der Landarbeiter an der Hausrückseite. »Sie sind sehr schön und völlig unberührt, deshalb wird es ziemlich anstrengend.«

Barbara and Thad Collum

Little Moose Lake, Adirondack Mountains, New York

Dans le nord de l'Etat de New York, près de la frontière canadienne, se dressent les monts Adirondacks, une région historique et idyllique de lacs et de forêts. Ce massif à la beauté hors du temps a été l'un des premiers aux Etats-Unis à réveiller les consciences en faveur de la protection de l'environnement. Des associations privées et des ligues d'architectes ont été créées pour limiter les constructions et contrôler le style architectural des résidences. De magnifiques demeures rustiques y sont cachées parmi les bouleaux et les pins et l'architecture traditionnelle d'Adirondacks du début du siècle – murs en épais rondins, intérieurs tout en bois taillés à la main, fer forgé artisanal – y est protégée. En 1915, un groupe d'amis, des anciens étudiants de l'université de Yale pour la plupart, construisirent une maison avec deux tourelles jumelles et un abri à bateau sur les rives du lac Little Moose («petit élan»). «C'est si beau ici, sans une âme dans les parages, qu'on a l'impression d'être aux portes du paradis», confie Barbara Collum qui, avec son mari Thad, en est aujourd'hui l'heureuse propriétaire.

In northern New York State, toward the Canadian border, there is a historic and Arcadian region of lakes and forests – the Adirondack Mountains. This panorama of pristine beauty was one of the earliest regions of the United States to have strong voices raised to guarantee preservation and protection. Private clubs and architectural leagues were formed to limit development, to control the architectural styles of residences. Great, rustic-style houses were hidden among the birches and pines, and the traditional turn-of-the-century Adirondack architecture – robust logs, hand-crafted timber interiors, hand-forged ironwork – is revered and preserved today. In 1915, on Little Moose Lake, a group of friends, many of them involved with Yale University, built a twin-turreted boathouse. "It's so beautiful there on the lake, with no-one in sight," said Barbara Collum, who now owns it with her husband, Thad. "You feel as if you can touch the sky."

Im Norden des Bundesstaats New York, in der Nähe der Grenze zu Kanada, liegen die Adirondack Mountains, eine historische und idyllische Landschaft mit unzähligen Seen und Wäldern. Diese abgelegene wunderschöne Region war eine der ersten in Amerika, in der Stimmen für striktere Naturschutzbestimmungen laut wurden. Um die weitere Erschließung zu begrenzen und die charakteristische Architektur der Häuser zu bewahren, wurden private Clubs und Zusammenschlüsse von Bauunternehmern gegründet. Typisch für die Adirondacks sind große, rustikale Gebäude, die versteckt zwischen Birken und Fichten liegen, und die traditionellen Stilelemente aus der Jahrhundertwende, die heute wieder geschätzt und erhalten werden: schwere Baumstämme, handgezimmerte Holzverkleidungen, handgeschmiedete Eisenverzierungen. 1915 baute eine Gruppe von Freunden, von denen viele von der Yale University kamen, am Little Moose Lake ein Bootshaus mit zwei Türmchen. »Es ist wunderschön hier am See, so ganz allein«, erzählt Barbara Collum, der dieses Bootshaus jetzt mit ihrem Mann Thad gehört. »Als könnte man den Himmel berühren.«

Previous pages: The Camp Collum boathouse, on Little Moose Lake, is surrounded by birch, spruce, pines and old hickory trees. On all of the 22 lakes of the Adirondack League Club, only one lake allows motorboats – the houses on its shores are only accessible by water. Thad hand-built the Adirondack guide boat seen in the boat storage shed. This traditional craft is especially lightweight for easy porterage.
Above, right and facing page: Historically, the distinctive log interiors were decorated with Adirondack furniture crafted in the winters by caretakers using left-over wood.

Double page précédente: La cabane des Collum, sur le lac Little Moose, est encerclée par les bouleaux, les épicéas, les pins et de vieux noyers blancs d'Amérique. Les bateaux à moteur ne sont autorisés que sur un seul des 22 lacs de l'Adirondack League Club. Les maisons au bord de l'eau ne sont accessibles que par bateau. Dans l'abri à bateaux, un canoë construit par Thad. Cette embarcation traditionnelle est particulièrement légère pour pouvoir être facilement hissée sur la terre ferme.
Ci-dessus, à droite et page de droite: Traditionnellement, les intérieurs en rondins typiques de la région étaient aménagés avec des meubles réalisés par les gardiens pendant l'hiver avec le bois non utilisé dans la construction.

Vorhergehende Doppelseite: Das Bootshaus der Collums am Little Moose Lake ist umgeben von Birken, Fichten, Kiefern und alten Hickorybäumen. Nur auf einem der ingesamt 22 Seen des Adirondack League Club sind Motorboote erlaubt – die Häuser an seinen Ufern sind nur vom Wasser aus zugänglich. Thad baute selbst das Ruderboot im Bootsschuppen. Diese traditionelle Bootsform wiegt besonders wenig, damit man sie an Land leichter tragen kann.
Oben, rechts und rechte Seite: Traditionellerweise werden die charakteristischen Blockhäuser mit Adirondack-Möbeln eingerichtet, die früher die Hausverwalter im Winter aus Holzresten fertigten.

Little Moose Lake, Adirondack Mountains, New York   Barbara and Thad Collum

Left and below: The separate sleep cabin is connected to the boathouse by a covered wooden walkway. The old bed is made of one full ironwood tree and a sapling. The sapling was used as a decorative headboard, its branches reaching for the ceiling. The footboard doubles as a useful bench. "This bed is incredibly comfortable," said Barbara Collum. "Everyone wants to sleep in it." The bunk beds, made for Thad and Barbara Collum's grandchildren, are crafted of white birch. The colorful bedcovers are authentic vintage blankets.

A gauche et ci-dessous: La cabane-chambre à coucher est reliée au reste de la bâtisse par une galerie surmontée d'un toit en bois. Le vieux lit est taillé dans un seul tronc de casuarina. Un autre arbre plus jeune fait office de tête de lit décorative, ses branches atteignant le plafond. Le repose-pied sert aussi de banquette. « Le lit est incroyablement confortable, tout le monde veut y dormir », assure Barbara Collum. Les lits superposés des petits-enfants de Thad et de Barbara ont été réalisés dans du bouleau blanc. Les dessus-de-lit colorés sont d'authentiques couvertures anciennes.

Links und unten: Die separate Schlafhütte ist mit dem Bootshaus durch einen überdachten Weg aus Holz verbunden. Das alte Bett wurde aus einem einzigen Eisenholzbaum und einem jungen Schössling gezimmert. Aus dem Schössling wurde ein dekoratives Kopfteil, seine Äste reichen bis an die Decke. Das verbreiterte Fußteil dient als praktische Bank. »Dieses Bett ist unglaublich bequem«, sagt Barbara Collum. »Jeder möchte darin schlafen.« Die Etagenbetten wurden für die Enkel von Barbara und Thad aus weißem Birkenholz gebaut. Die farbenprächtigen Bettüberwürfe sind Originaldecken aus der Gegend.

Facing page: On the polished hardwood floor, left, is a rare ironwood cellaret crafted in 1915 for the camp's libations. The lower shelf, lead-lined, was used to hold chunks of ice. "The living room is sunny and bright throughout the day," said Barbara Collum, who is a decorator. "We love to go up to the lake, and think nothing of driving three hours just to stay there overnight. Every season there is glorious."

Page de gauche: A gauche, sur le plancher en bois dur poli, une curiosité: un cabinet à liqueurs en bois-de-fer réalisé en 1915 pour les occupants des lieux. L'étagère inférieure, tapissée de plomb, servait à conserver des éclats de glace. « La salle de séjour est inondée de soleil toute la journée » affirme Barbara Colum, qui est décoratrice. « Nous adorons monter au lac et n'hésitons jamais à faire les trois heures de route en voiture rien que pour y passer une nuit. Chaque saison y est superbe ».

Linke Seite: Auf dem polierten Hartholzfußboden steht links ein seltenes Weinschränkchen aus Eisenholz, das sich 1915 die Zecher des Camps anfertigen ließen. Im unteren, mit Blei ausgeschlagenen Fach wurden Eiswürfel aufbewahrt. »Das Wohnzimmer ist den ganzen Tag über hell und sonnig«, erzählt Barbara Collum, die als Dekorateurin arbeitet. »Wir lieben den See und es macht uns nichts aus, drei Stunden mit dem Auto zu fahren, nur um hier die Nacht zu verbringen. Hier ist es zu jeder Jahreszeit wundervoll.«

Russel Wright

Garrison, Hudson River Valley, New York

Pour Russel Wright et sa famille, se réfugier à Manitoga, leur domaine de 40 hectares à une heure de Manhattan dans la nature sauvage de la vallée de l'Hudson, était un véritable rituel. Wright découvrit Manitoga («Demeure du grand esprit» dans la langue de la tribu algonquine qui vivait là autrefois) en 1942 et des membres de sa famille habitent encore sur la propriété. Célébré comme le premier grand designer industriel américain, Russel Wright (1904–1976) a créé des lignes entières de vaisselle en aluminium filé et en céramique, des radios en mélamine et des meubles modulaires qui comptent aujourd'hui parmi les objets les plus recherchés des collectionneurs. Il a déclaré: «Comment peut-on s'accrocher aux traditions à une époque où tout change si vite et si radicalement? Pour nous adapter à cette grande révolution sociale, nous devons naturellement traverser une période de transition. Grâce à l'industrie, nous avons atteint un degré de confort à grande échelle auquel aucune civilisation n'avait encore jamais accédé.» Manitoga devint sa retraite, un lieu où la nature nourrissait son âme.

Escaping to Manitoga, their 80-acre estate an hour from Manhattan in the wilds of the Hudson River Valley, was a special ritual for designer Russel Wright and his family. Wright first discovered Manitoga (Home of the Great Spirit in the native Algonquin language) in 1942 and members of his family still live on the property. Revered as the first major American industrial designer, Russel Wright (1904–1976) created mid-century modern collections of spun aluminum and pottery tableware, melamine radios and modular furniture that are among today's hottest collectibles. He asked, "How can you hold on to traditions in times that are changing so fast and so radically? In adapting ourselves to this big social revolution we are naturally going through a transition period. Fed by industry we have accomplished greater comfort on a larger scale than any previous civilization." Manitoga became his refuge, a place where nature fed his soul.

Für den Designer Russel Wright und seine Familie bedeuteten die Ausflüge nach Manitoga, einen Besitz von 30 Hektar in der Wildnis des Hudson River Valley, immer ein ganz besonderes Ritual. Wright entdeckte 1942 Manitoga, in der Sprache der Algonquin bedeutet das »Ort des Großen Geistes«. Angehörige seiner Familie leben heute noch dort. Russel Wright (1904–1976) gilt als der erste wichtige amerikanische Industriedesigner und schuf in den 1950ern Objekte aus gesponnenem Aluminium, Keramikgeschirr, Melaminradios und modulare Möbel, die heute begehrte Sammlerstücke sind. »Wieso sollte man an Traditionen festhalten, wenn sich alles so schnell und radikal ändert?« fragte er. »Wir müssen uns an die Übergangszeit anpassen, in der wir leben und die durch die große soziale Revolution ausgelöst wurde. Die moderne Industrieproduktion hat für alle einen größeren Komfort bewirkt als jede andere Zivilisation vor uns.« Manitoga wurde der Zufluchtsort von Russel Wright, ein Ort, an dem er sich von der Natur inspirieren ließ.

Facing page: In his retreat, which he called Dragon Rock, Wright seemed to escape to an earlier era of handhewn rocks, noble timbers, and the ideals of living in total harmony with nature. In the bathroom, rocks seem to have tumbled indoors and the Murano-glass mosaic bath seems temporary, at best, until nature takes over.

Page de droite: Dans sa retraite, qu'il appelait «le rocher du dragon», Wright semblait faire un retour en arrière à un âge où les pierres étaient taillées à la main, les bois étaient nobles et l'on vivait en totale harmonie avec la nature. Dans la salle de bains, les rochers semblent s'être déversés à l'intérieur et la baignoire en mosaïque de verre de Murano sur le point d'être envahie par la végétation.

Rechte Seite: In seinem Refugium, das er selbst »Dragon Rock« nannte, ließ Wright mit handbehauenen Felsen und massiven Holzbalken eine weit zurückliegende Ära wieder aufleben, in der das Leben in harmonischem Einklang mit der Natur verlief. Im Badezimmer scheinen die Felsbrocken gerade eben zur Tür hereingefallen zu sein und das Mosaikbad aus Muranoglas hat wohl nur so lange Bestand, bis die Natur wieder die Oberhand gewinnt.

First pages and previous pages: Early apostles of ecology, the Wrights animated the self-effacing architecture with massive stones and timbers. They diverted a stream to form graceful waterfalls, and gave the house large panels of glass to make it almost invisible. Working with architect David Leavitt, Wright dreamed up a house, now venerated in America's National Register of Historic Places. Manitoga nestles so closely into the granite outcrop that at times it feels as if the rocks are encroaching into the rooms.
Above and right: The wall panels are inspired by Japanese Shoji paper screens.

Premières pages et doubles pages précédentes: Ecologistes avant l'heure, les Wright animaient leur architecture discrète de pierres et de poutres massives. Ils détournèrent un ruisseau pour créer des cascades et équipèrent leur vaste demeure de cloisons de verre pour la rendre presque invisible. Avec l'aide de l'architecte David Leavitt, Wright a conçu la maison de ses rêves, aujourd'hui classée monument historique. Manitoga est nichée si près d'un affleurement de granit qu'on a parfois l'impression que la roche cherche à s'immiscer dans les pièces.
Ci-dessus et à droite: Les écrans sont inspirés des shoji japonais en papier.

Eingangsseiten und vorhergehende Doppelseiten: Als frühe Vertreter der ökologischen Bewegung gestalteten die Wrights eine zurückhaltende Architektur mit Massivsteinen und Holzbalken. Aus einem umgeleiteten Bach wurde ein Wasserfall und die großen Fensterflächen lassen das Haus geradezu unsichtbar werden. Mit dem Architekten David Leavitt entwarf Wright ein wunderbares Haus, das jetzt in das amerikanische National Register of Historic Places aufgenommen wurde. Manitoga schmiegt sich so eng an die Granitfelswand, dass es zuweilen scheint, als ob der Stein in die Räume vordringt.
Oben und rechts: Die Trennwände sind inspiriert von japanischen Shoji-Papierparavents.

Ruth and Costantino Nivola

East Hampton, Long Island, New York

*Peu de maisons ressemblent autant à leurs occupants que celle-ci, ha-
bitée par un couple remarquable depuis plus de 50 ans. Ruth Nivola,
qui a grandi à Munich, a rencontré son mari Tino, un Sarde, lorsqu'ils
étaient tous les deux étudiants en art à Monza, près de Milan. Leur
professeur de sculpture s'appelait Marino Marini. Ils se sont mariés en
1938, avant de mettre le cap sur l'Amérique l'année suivante. A la fin
de 1947, ils ont acheté cette petite maison en bois près d'East Hampton. Construite en 1754, elle était bordée de cèdres qui rappelaient à
Tino sa chère Italie natale. «Bâtie par des agriculteurs, elle était en
ruines» se souvient Ruth. «Nous l'avons remodelée, avons abattu des
murs, l'avons aérée». Au fil des ans, le couple y a ajouté un atelier de
sculpture où Tino pouvait travailler le travertin, le bois, le bronze et
poncer ses bas-reliefs en plâtre. «Les fermiers qui ont construit cette
maison savaient ce qu'ils faisaient», confie Ruth. «Elle capte la lumière toute la journée. Comme elle est entourée de forêts, elle est très
paisible».*

This house, perhaps more than most, is a portrait of the remarkable couple who have lived there for more than 50 years. Ruth
Nivola, who grew up in Munich, met her husband, Tino, originally
from Sardinia, when they were art students together in Monza,
near Milan. They studied sculpture with Marino Marini. The two
married in 1938, and sailed for New York the following year. At the
end of 1947, the couple acquired a small shingled house near East
Hampton. Built in 1754, it was surrounded by cedars which re-
minded Tino of his beloved Italy. "The house, built by farmers,
was in ruins," recalled Ruth. "We remodeled it, tore down walls,
opened it up." Over the years the couple added a sculpture studio
where Tino crafted in travertine marble, wood, and bronze, and he
sand-cast plaster bas reliefs. "The farmers who built the house
had a great sense of site placement," said Ruth. "It catches the
light all day. And it's surrounded by woodland, so it's very peaceful."

*Dieses Haus ist vielleicht mehr als andere ein Spiegelbild des unge-
wöhnlichen Paares, das hier über 50 Jahre wohnte. Ruth Nivola
wuchs in München auf und lernte den gebürtigen Sarden Tino ken-
nen, als sie gemeinsam bei Marino Marini in Monza Bildhauerei stu-
dierten. 1938 heirateten sie und schifften sich ein Jahr später nach
New York ein. Ende 1947 kauften sie ein kleines, mit Schindeln verkleidetes Haus in der Nähe von East Hampton. Das Gebäude stammt
von 1754 und lag mitten in einem Zedernhain, was Tino an sein ge-
liebtes Italien erinnerte. »Das Haus war ursprünglich von Farmern
gebaut worden«, erinnert sich Ruth. »Anfangs war es eine einzige
Ruine. Wir bauten es um, rissen Wände ein, machten es großzügiger.« Im Lauf der Jahre kam ein Bildhaueratelier hinzu, in dem Tino
an Skulpturen aus Travertin-Marmor, Holz und Bronze arbeitete und
Bas-Reliefs aus Gips schuf. »Die Farmer, die das Haus erbauten, hatten viel Gespür für den richtigen Ort«, sagt Ruth. »Den ganzen Tag
fällt helles Licht ein und es ist gleichzeitig von Bäumen umgeben, so
dass es hier sehr friedlich ist.«*

Le Corbusier
1er octobre
50

Facing page and above: Tino and Ruth Nivola met and befriended architect Le Corbusier. "In October 1950, when he was returning home, via New York, from South America, he stayed with us for a few days," recalled Ruth. "One day he said, 'it's a lovely house but it needs a mural.' It's painted directly onto the plaster. And it has given us both such pleasure for half a century." They preferred to keep the rooms and the studio simple and austere – but rich in memories.
Following pages: Sadly Tino died 12 years ago, but Ruth has left his studio exactly as it was. Now art students and art lovers come to visit.

Page de gauche et ci-dessus: Tino et Ruth Nivola ont rencontré l'architecte Le Corbusier avec lequel ils sont devenus amis. «En octobre 1950, alors qu'il rentrait d'Amérique du Sud en passant par New York, il a séjourné chez nous quelques jours», se souvient Ruth. «Un jour, il nous a dit: ‹C'est une maison charmante mais il lui manque une fresque.› Il l'a peinte directement sur le plâtre. Elle nous apporte beaucoup de plaisir depuis un demi-siècle.» Les Nivola ont préféré garder les pièces et l'atelier simples et assez austères, mais riches en souvenirs.
Double page suivante: Tino est mort il y a 12 ans, mais Ruth a gardé son atelier. Aujourd'hui, des étudiants et des amateurs d'art viennent régulièrement se former ici.

Linke Seite und oben: Als ihr Freund, der Architekt Le Corbusier, im Oktober 1950 von Südamerika via New York nach Hause fuhr, blieb er ein paar Tage bei Tino und Ruth. »Eines Tages«, erinnert sich Ruth, »meinte er, dies sei zwar ein hübsches Haus, aber ihm fehle ein Wandgemälde. Und er malte eines direkt auf den weißen Mörtel. Seit einem halben Jahrhundert haben wir viel Freude daran.« Tino und Ruth richteten die Räume und das Atelier schlicht, fast nüchtern ein, aber sie sind reich an Erinnerungen.
Folgende Doppelseite: Tino starb vor 12 Jahren, aber sein Atelier blieb unverändert. Heute besuchen es Kunststudenten.

Joanne Creveling and Frank Lookstein

Shelter Island, Long Island, New York

A Manhattan, les étés sont sans pitié. La chaleur et l'humidité vous grillent le cerveau et ramollissent votre créativité. La seule issue est de fuir, et vite. C'est pourquoi tous les vendredis, vers midi, l'exode commence. La plupart des fuyards expérimentés mettent le cap sur les plages bondées de Long Island, mais les plus aventureux cherchent le salut plus loin, dans de petites villes de la côte et les îles désertes (ou presque). C'est à North Folk, sur Long Island, que Joanne Creveling, grande publiciste spécialisée dans le design et les antiquités, venait passer ses vacances quand elle était enfant. Elle se souvient encore de ses séjours idylliques dans la maison de ses grands-parents, d'où on apercevait Shelter Island au loin dans la baie. Vingt ans plus tard, elle a redécouvert l'île avec son mari Frank Lookstein et leurs deux fils. Ils ont déniché une maison victorienne en bois, conçue à l'origine par Calvert Vaux comme un centre de colonie de vacances méthodiste. «Je voulais que le décor soit apaisant et monochrome », se souvient Creveling. Son thème estival se décline tout en blanc et crème.

Summers in Manhattan are brutal. Heat and humidity sizzle the brain and fizzle creativity. The best revenge is a fast escape, and on Friday afternoons around lunchtime the exodus begins. Many escape artists head for the crowded beaches of Long Island, but dedicated adventurers look further afield to small towns and (almost) undiscovered islands. It was to the North Fork of Long Island that Joanne Creveling, now a leading publicist specializing in design and antiques, was sent as a child. Staying with her grandparents was like heaven, she recalled, with magical Shelter Island out in the bay. Twenty years later Creveling, with her husband, Frank Lookstein, and their two sons rediscovered Shelter Island. They found a board-and-batten Victorian house, designed by Calvert Vaux, and originally built for a Methodist summer camp. "I wanted the decor to be as restful and monochromatic as possible," recalled Creveling. White and cream became her summer theme.

Die Sommer in Manhattan sind brutal. Hitze und Schwüle setzen einem zu und lähmen jede Kreativität. Das beste Mittel dagegen ist die Flucht ins Freie, und freitagnachmittags, nach dem Mittagessen, beginnt der Exodus. Die meisten zieht es zu den überfüllten Stränden von Long Island, aber echte Abenteurer halten Ausschau nach weiter draußen liegenden kleineren Orten und (fast) noch unberührten Inseln. Joanne Creveling, eine bekannte Publizistin mit Schwerpunkt Design und Antiquitäten, wurde als Kind im Sommer immer nach North Fork auf Long Island geschickt. Die Ferien bei den Großeltern waren himmlisch, erinnert sie sich, besonders wegen der magischen Shelter Island, draußen in der Bucht. Zwanzig Jahre später entdeckte Creveling Shelter Island neu, diesmal mit ihrem Mann Frank Lookstein und ihren beiden Söhnen. Sie fanden dort ein Holzhaus im viktorianischen Stil, das von Calvert Vaux entworfen und ursprünglich als Sommercamp der Methodisten gebaut worden war. »Die Einrichtung sollte so ruhig und monochrom wie möglich sein«, sagt Creveling. Weiß und Creme wurden zu ihrem Sommerthema.

Previous pages: On hot summer afternoons, the verandah welcomes friends and visitors from nearby towns.
Above: The family "inherited" a lifetime's assortment of indifferent furniture with the house. Creveling's solution to the jumble: paint them all white to create harmony and light.
Right: Creveling has transformed a rather forlorn screened-in porch into the most popular room in the house. It's here that Sunday papers and stacks of magazines are read, and orange juice poured.

Premières pages: Les chauds après-midi d'été, la famille et les amis venus des villes voisines se réfugient sur la véranda.
Ci-dessus: Avec la maison, la famille a «hérité» d'un assortiment disparate de meubles quelconques. Creveling a trouvé la solution pour les harmoniser: les peindre tous en blanc pour apporter de la lumière.
A droite: Creveling a transformé un porche tristounet en pièce la plus prisée de la maison. C'est ici qu'on lit les journaux du dimanche et qu'on feuillette des piles de magazines devant des cruches de jus d'orange frais.

Vorhergehende Doppelseite: An heißen Sommernachmittagen treffen sich Freunde und Besucher aus den nahe gelegenen Orten auf der Veranda.
Oben: Die Familie erbte zusammen mit dem Haus eine Sammlung unterschiedlichster Möbel. Die Lösung: Creveling strich sie alle weiß, um das Haus hell und harmonisch erscheinen zu lassen.
Rechts: Die früher etwas verloren wirkende überdachte Veranda ist heute der beliebteste Platz im Haus: Hier liest man bei einem Glas frisch gepressten Orangensaft die Sonntagszeitung und ganze Stapel von Zeitschriften.

Shelter Island, Long Island, New York   Joanne Creveling and Frank Lookstein

Shelter Island days are quiet and dreamy, with just a few events like midsummer fireworks and arts and crafts shows to break the spell. On the enclosed porch, in the garden, and in each room, Joanne unified the decor with white paint, white linens, and collections of old etchings. Joanne likes the ease of seagrass matting.

Sur Shelter Island, les jours s'écoulent tranquilles et songeurs. Seuls les feux d'artifices du mois d'août et les foires à la brocante viennent perturber cette quiétude. Sous le porche clos, dans le jardin et dans chaque pièce, elle a unifié le décor avec de la peinture blanche, du lin blanc et des collections de gravures anciennes. Joanne aime le confort et l'odeur des tapis en jonc de mer.

Die Tage auf Shelter Island vergehen ruhig und friedlich, nur ab und zu gibt es ein Mittsommernachtsfeuer oder Jahrmärkte, die den Zauber stören. Verschiedene Weißstöne, weißes Leinen und alte Kupferstiche geben der Veranda, dem Garten und jedem Raum ein harmonisches Gesamtbild. Joanne liebt die Behaglichkeit der Seegrasmatten.

Shelter Island, Long Island, New York

Joanne Creveling and Frank Lookstein

The massive old oak dining table was given, lickety split, multiple coats of glossy white paint. The simple wooden, caned dining chairs had been used in the late 1800s in the prayer chapel of the Methodist meeting room.

En deux coups de cuillère à pot, la massive table en chêne s'est retrouvée badigeonnée de plusieurs couches de peinture blanche satinée. Les

sobres chaises cannées en bois étaient utilisées à la fin du 19ᵉ siècle dans la chapelle de la salle commune méthodiste.

Der massive Esstisch aus alter Eiche wurde in rascher Folge mehrere Male mit Schichten glänzender weißer Farbe gestrichen. Die schlichten Holzstühle mit Rohrgeflechtsitzfläche standen um 1800 in der Kapelle des Versammlungsraums der Methodisten.

Upstairs bedrooms in the house continue Creveling's deftly edited
"blanc de Chine" refrain. Here, floors, walls and ceilings were all
painted satiny white and mirrors were hung to catch light. Vintage
linens add couture panache to beds and pillows.

Dans les chambres situées à l'étage, Creveling a poursuivi son thème
blanc de Chine. Ici, les sols, les murs et les plafonds ont tous été peints
en blanc satiné, tandis que des miroirs jouent avec la lumière. Les
draps anciens confèrent une note très «couture» aux lits et aux
oreillers.

In den Schlafzimmern im Obergeschoss setzte Creveling ihre Weiß-in-
Weiß-Komposition fort. Böden, Decken und Wände sind alle Satin-
weiß gestrichen, die Spiegel reflektieren das einfallende Licht. Antike
Leinenstoffe verleihen den Betten und Kissen eine elegante Note.

Shelter Island, Long Island, New York　　　　**Joanne Creveling and Frank Lookstein**

Berns Fry and Ricks Lee

East Hampton, Long Island, New York

Pour les estivants de Manhattan en quête de soleil, la ville d'East Hampton sur Long Island a beaucoup à offrir, mais ce n'est pas l'endroit idéal pour fuir la métropole. Le jeune décorateur new-yorkais Berns Fry a néanmoins trouvé le moyen de s'installer à un jet de pierre des antiquaires d'East Hampton tout en profitant de la vie tranquille et du bon air de la campagne. Il y a trois ans, avec son compagnon Ricks Lee, paysagiste, ils ont déniché une charmante maison en bois avec trois chambres à coucher. Construite en 1985 dans la forêt, c'est une interprétation moderne de l'architecture traditionnelle de Nouvelle-Angleterre. Fry a illuminé les murs de blanc crémeux tandis que Lee plantait des plantes à croissance rapide telles que des cosmos et du chèvrefeuille. «Auparavant, j'avais toujours vécu dans des maisons anciennes. On voulait effacer le côté neuf», explique Fry. Traditionnellement, la maison n'était habitée qu'en juin, juillet et août, mais maintenant le couple y habite la moitié de la semaine, travaillant à la fois pour des clients à Manhattan et dans les Hamptons.

For Manhattan's summer sunseekers, the town of East Hampton on Long Island offers rich fare – but little real escape from the intensities of the metropolis. Young New York interior designer Berns Fry has found a way to be within whistling distance of East Hampton's antiques dealers, and still enjoy a relaxed and breezy country life. Three years ago, he and his partner, Ricks Lee, a landscape designer, found a charming three-bedroom, cedar-shingle house in the woods. Built in 1985, it is a modern interpretation of traditional salt-box architecture. Fry polished up the interior with creamy-white paint, and Lee cultivated fast-growing plants like cosmos and honeysuckle to give their new digs a little history. "I've always lived in old houses before," said Fry. "We wanted to take away the newness." The house was originally a June, July, August escape from the city. Now the partners divide their year-round work weeks – half in Manhattan and half in the Hamptons.

Den Sonnenhungrigen aus Manhattan bietet East Hampton auf Long Island viel, nur keine echte Alternative zum hektischen Großstadtleben. Der junge New Yorker Interior-Designer Berns Fry hat eine Möglichkeit gefunden, ganz in der Nähe der Antiquitätenhändler von East Hampton zu wohnen und gleichzeitig entspanntes Landleben zu genießen. Vor drei Jahren entdeckten er und sein Partner, der Landschaftsarchitekt Ricks Lee, in den Wäldern ein bezauberndes, mit Schindeln aus Zedernholz verkleidetes Haus. Es wurde 1985 erbaut, verfügt über drei Schlafzimmer und ist eine moderne Interpretation der traditionellen »Salt-box«-Architektur der Ostküste. Fry strich das Innere in einem cremig-weißen Ton und Lee pflanzte schnell wachsende Pflanzen wie Kosmos oder Geißblatt, um das Haus etwas älter wirken zu lassen. »Ich hatte bisher immer in alten Häusern gelebt«, sagt Fry. »Wir wollten, dass es nicht so neu aussieht.« Ursprünglich wurde das Haus nur in den Sommermonaten von Juni bis August genutzt, doch heute leben und arbeiten die beiden wochenweise in Manhattan und draußen in den Hamptons.

First pages: At the East Hampton house, Ella the mixed-breed mutt takes some rays on an antique Adirondack chair. "We got her from the animal rescue league the day Ella Fitzgerald died, so we named her Ella," Fry explained.
Above and right: Centuries of design history are illustrated in the living room, which includes an original "Butterfly" chair, a Louis-Seize-style bench, 1930s patio chairs, new cubistic metal tables, a Regency mirror, and Victorian finials.
Facing page: Vintage galvanized metal dining chairs, painted white, surround an old art student's desk.

Premières pages: Dans sa maison de East Hampton, Ella – au pedigree incertain – prend le soleil sur une chaise ancienne d'Adirondacks. «On l'a baptisée ainsi parce qu'on l'a trouvée dans un refuge le jour de la mort d'Ella Fitzgerald» explique Fry.
Ci-dessus et à droite: Dans le salon, plusieurs siècles d'histoire du design vous contemplent, notamment une authentique chaise Butterfly, un banc de style Louis XVI, des chaises de jardin des années 1930, des tables néo-cubistes, un miroir Regency et des fleurons victoriens.
Page de droite: Des chaises anciennes en métal galvanisé, repeintes en blanc, entourent un ancien bureau d'étudiant en art.

Erste Doppelseite: Die Mischlingshündin Ella sitzt auf einem antiken Adirondack-Stuhl in der Sonne. »Wir bekamen sie an dem Tag, an dem Ella Fitzgerald starb; deshalb heißt sie Ella«, erklärt Fry.
Oben und rechts: Mehrere Jahrhunderte sind hier im Wohnzimmer versammelt: vom originalen »Butterfly«-Stuhl über eine Bank im Louis-seize-Stil, Patio-Stühle aus den 1930ern, neue Metalltische im kubistischen Stil, einen Regency-Spiegel bis hin zu viktorianischen Ornamenten.
Rechte Seite: Weiß gestrichene Esszimmerstühle aus galvanisiertem Metall stehen an einem alten Schultisch.

Facing page: *A pair of flea market tables, by an unknown designer, are among Fry's favorite objects. "I like their strict angularity," he said. "They're one of the few contemporary designs in the house.*
Above and right: *The bedrooms are also repositories for Fry and Lee's ever-changing treasures and trophies. The gold-bordered bedcover was made from a tablecloth found at the famous 26th Street flea market in New York City. Fry appreciates wicker and wood and gilding that show signs of life, of wear, of history. "Old things are always more soulful and beautiful than shiny new things," he said.*

Page de gauche : *parmi les objets favoris de Fry, cette paire de petites tables dénichées aux Puces, œuvre d'un designer non identifié. «J'aime leurs angles stricts. Elles comptent parmi les rares créations contemporaines de la maison.»*
Ci-dessus et à droite : *Les chambres servent également à entreposer les trésors et trophées de Fry et de Lee. Le dessus-de-lit bordé d'or a été réalisé avec une nappe chinée sur le célèbre marché aux puces de la 26e rue à Manhattan. Fry aime l'osier, le bois et les dorures qui portent des traces de vie, d'usure et d'histoire. «Les vieilleries ont toujours plus d'âme et de charme que les objets flambant neufs».*

Linke Seite: *Das Tischpaar von einem unbekannten Designer gehört zu Frys Lieblingsobjekten, er fand es auf einem Flohmarkt. »Mir gefällt die strenge eckige Form«, meint er. »Sie gehören zu den wenigen modernen Designobjekten in diesem Haus.«*
Oben und rechts: *In den Schlafzimmern werden die ständig wechselnden Sammlungen von Fry und Lee aufbewahrt. Die Bettdecke mit Goldborte wurde aus einer Tischdecke genäht, die sie auf dem berühmten New Yorker Flohmarkt in der 26th Street entdeckten. Fry liebt Korbwaren, Holz und Vergoldungen, denen man ihr Alter ansieht: »Alte Dinge haben immer mehr Ausstrahlung und sind interessanter als nagelneue Sachen.«*

Susan and Howard Kaminsky

Sharon, Connecticut

Quel enfant n'en a pas rêvé? C'est un clin d'œil à Peter Pan, un coup de chapeau aux frères Grimm, le tout enveloppé dans l'étreinte aérienne d'un érable centenaire. Les Kaminsky – il édite, elle écrit – vivent à Manhattan et passent leurs week-ends dans le nord-ouest du Connecticut dans une ravissante maison en bois datant de 1740. «J'ai toujours rêvé d'avoir une cabane dans les arbres», se souvient Howard. «J'ai cherché le bon arbre sur notre propriété et suis tombé sur ce splendide érable au milieu d'un champ». Les Kaminsky ont chargé le décorateur John Ryman de leur créer un petit nid digne d'Hansel et Gretel. Une robuste plate-forme a d'abord été hissée en équilibre à quatre mètres au-dessus du sol, suivie par des fenêtres, des portes et des cloisons en bois ancien récupérées sur d'autres sites. Il n'y a pas l'électricité mais la maisonnette est habitable et douillette huit mois par an. «Même par vent fort, elle reste inébranlable», assure Howard. «Dedans, on écrit, on lit, on contemple les prés tout autour». Bref, ils se fondent dans la nature tels des esprits arboricoles.

This is every child's dream – a wink at Peter Pan, a nod at the Brothers Grimm – all wrapped in the aerial embrace of a 100-year-old maple tree. The Kaminskys – he's a publisher and she is an author – live in Manhattan and spend weekends in a gracious 1740 shingled house in Northwest Connecticut. "I had always wanted a tree house," recalled Howard. "I looked around our property for the right tree, and found this splendid maple tree in the middle of a field." The Kaminskys engaged designer John Ryman to conjure up their Hansel and Gretel house. Balanced 20 feet in the air, Ryman's sturdy platform went up first, and then he crafted the windows, doors and walls of old, recycled architectural salvage and timbers. The snug little cottage is cozy for eight months of the year. "Even in strong winds, the tree house does not budge," said Howard. "We write, we read, we gaze out over the meadows." Briefly, they are a part of nature, arboreal spirits.

So sieht ein Kindertraum aus: ein bisschen Peter Pan, ein bisschen Gebrüder Grimm – und das Ganze eingehüllt in die luftige Umarmung eines 100 Jahre alten Ahornbaums. Die Kaminskys leben in Manhattan, er ist Verleger und sie Autorin. Die Wochenenden verbringen sie jedoch in einem zauberhaften, mit Schindeln verkleideten Haus von 1740 im Norden von Connecticut. »Ich wollte schon immer ein Baumhaus haben«, erinnert sich Howard. »Und so hielt ich auf unserem Grundstück Ausschau nach einem geeigneten Baum und stieß auf diesen herrlichen Ahorn mitten auf einem Feld.« Die Kaminskys beauftragten den Designer John Ryman, ihr Hänsel-und-Gretel-Haus zu entwerfen. Zunächst befestigte Ryman eine stabile Plattform in der luftigen Höhe von sechs Metern, danach baute er die Fenster, Türen und Wände – alles aus altem Holz und Materialien, die aus verfallenen Gebäuden gerettet worden waren. Es gibt kein elektrisches Licht, aber das kleine Cottage bietet acht Monate im Jahr ein gemütliches Zuhause. »Es hält sogar starkem Wind stand«, erzählt Howard. »Hier schreiben wir, lesen und blicken über die Wiesen.« Dann sind sie für kurze Zeit Teil der Natur, Baumgeister.

First page and facing page: Howard and Susan walk through the late-summer meadow and make the easy climb into their magic kingdom. The vintage Olivetti typewriter on the desk is just for fun: both Howard and Susan write their books by hand. "I love it here in the spring when the light is brighter," noted Howard. "And in summer, even when it's warm, we catch the breezes as they waft through the branches." In autumn, golden leaves alight on the roof and flutter past the windows.

Première page et page de gauche: Par une belle journée de fin d'été, Howard et Susan traversent le pré pour grimper dans leur royaume magique. La vieille machine à écrire Olivetti sur le bureau est purement décorative: Howard et Susan rédigent leurs textes à la main. «J'adore être ici au printemps quand la lumière est la plus forte», observe Howard. «L'été, même quand il fait chaud, nous profitons des brises qui filtrent à travers les branches». A l'automne, les feuilles dorées tapissent le toit et passent en virevoltant devant les fenêtres.

Eingangsseite und linke Seite: Howard und Susan auf dem Weg durch die spätsommerliche Wiese hinauf in ihr luftiges Reich. Die alte Olivetti-Schreibmaschine auf dem Schreibtisch ist nur Dekoration: Howard und Susan schreiben ihre Manuskripte per Hand. »Besonders gern bin ich im Frühling hier, wenn es heller ist«, erzählt Howard. »Im Sommer, selbst wenn es warm ist, gibt es hier oben zwischen den Zweigen immer einen kühlen Lufthauch.« Im Herbst flattert goldenes Laub auf das Dach und an den Fenstern vorbei.

Above and left: Designer John Ryman created an atmospheric little cottage, complete with bamboo shades, quirky old timbers, and the charm of antique doors and windows. The 1890 "cannonball" daybed, dressed with striped cotton ticking, is pillowed for impromptu afternoon naps. "Perhaps best of all, John left the tree trunk rough and rustic. You really do feel as if you live in a tree – a tree with a wonderful spirit and soul."

Ci-dessus et à gauche: Le décorateur John Ryman a créé une vraie cabane de charme, avec ses volets en bambou, ses bois noueux, ses portes et fenêtres anciennes. Le lit de repos «boulets de canon» de 1890, tapissé d'une robuste toile à matelas rayée, est prêt pour les siestes impromptues. «John a laissé le tronc tel quel, brut et rustique, si bien qu'on a vraiment l'impression de vivre dans un arbre, un arbre à l'âme et l'esprit merveilleux».

Oben und links: Der Designer John Ryman schuf ein stimmungsvolles kleines Cottage, mit Bambus-Jalousien, skurril geformten Ästen und dem Charme alter Türen und Fenster. Die Kissen und das Tagesbett von 1890 mit den gedrechselten Pfosten sind mit einem gestreiften Baumwolldrillich bezogen und laden zur Siesta ein. »Das Beste ist vielleicht, dass John den Baumstamm nicht bearbeitet hat. So hat man das Gefühl, wirklich in einem Baum zu leben – einem wundervollen und beseelten Baum.«

James Rose

Ridgewood, Delaware River, New Jersey

James C. Rose (1913–1991), paysagiste, écrivain, rebelle et disciple du bouddhisme zen, a créé pour lui et sa famille une maison et un jardin d'esprit moderne qu'il a entretenus en état d'évolution perpétuelle pendant plus de 40 ans. Cette œuvre, sans doute la plus significative de ce créateur de jardins et de cet aménageur de sites anticonformiste, est désormais inscrite au registre des monuments historiques. «Rose était infatigable, toujours en train d'expérimenter et de chercher à re-définir l'essence du jardin américain moderne» observe Dean Cardasis, directeur du James Rose Center. Aujourd'hui, plus d'une décennie après sa mort, la propriété permet aux spécialistes de l'histoire du design d'étudier toute la richesse de la pensée, des motivations, des improvisations, de l'architecture et de la philosophie de Rose, qu'il a ex-primée ici pendant un demi-siècle. Il considérait que le paysage environnant devait faire partie intégrante de la maison. De fait, celle-ci est plutôt petite, mais le jardin et les bassins qui l'entourent brouillent les frontières et la font paraître infinie.

Landscape designer, writer, rebel, disciple of Zen Buddhism, James C. Rose (1913–1991) created a modernist house and garden for himself and his family, then worked on it, and kept it in a state of perpetual evolution for more than 40 years. The house is by far the most significant work of this maverick garden designer and site planner, and it is now on the National Register of Historic Places. "Rose was a restless spirit, always experimenting and searching for meaning in the modern American garden," noted Dean Cardasis, the director of the James Rose Center. Today, more than a decade after his death, the property provides for design historians a rich expression of half a century of Rose's thought, motivation, design improvisations, architecture, and philosophy. Rose believed in making the landscape an integral part of the house. The house is, in fact, quite small, noted Cardasis, but the garden and pools and blurring of boundaries make it feel infinite.

Der Landschaftsarchitekt, Schriftsteller, Rebell und Anhänger des Zen-Buddhismus James C. Rose (1913–1991) gestaltete für sich und seine Familie dieses modernistische Haus, setzte die Arbeit daran be-ständig fort und hielt es mehr als 40 Jahre in einem Zustand stetiger Entwicklung. Das Haus ist das wichtigste Werk dieses ungestümen Ar-chitektur- und Gartenbauvisionärs und wurde jetzt in das amerikani-sche National Register of Historic Places aufgenommen. »Rose war ein ruheloser Geist, er experimentierte ständig und war auf der Suche nach einer neuen Bedeutung im modernen amerikanischen Garten-design«, meint Dean Cardasis, Direktor des James Rose Center. Mehr als zehn Jahre nach seinem Tod wird hier für alle Designfans die Ge-dankenwelt von James Rose erfahrbar, seine Beweggründe, Architek-turideen, spontanen Einfälle und die Lebensphilosophie, die ihn ein halbes Jahrhundert lang bewegten. Der Garten war für ihn integraler Bestandteil des Hauses. Sein eigenes Haus war eigentlich ziemlich klein, wie Cardasis anmerkt, aber es gibt keine klare Grenze zum Gar-ten mit seinen Teichen, deshalb wirkt es offen und weit.

Left: Rose's aim was the total fusion between the created landscape and the built world. Rooms were positioned to view and experience nature directly. Rose designed everything in his house, including this organic sofa and table crafted from scrap metal and found wood.
Facing page: Harmony, silence, and simplicity were at the core of James Rose's credo. Rose meditated twice a day in his Zendo, often with the specific goal of clearing his mind of design preconceptions. He liked to approach each day with a free and open creative spirit, he said. In the ceiling, Rose created a silhouette image of a Zen student genuflecting to his master, out of wood and fibreglass.

A gauche: Rose voulait marier le paysage aménagé et le monde construit. Les pièces sont toutes orientées de sorte à voir et vivre directement la nature. Rose a dessiné tout de ce qui se trouve dans la maison, y compris le canapé organique et la table, réalisés avec des morceaux de métal et de bois récupérés dans la nature.
Page de droite: L'harmonie, le silence et la simplicité étaient au cœur des préoccupations de Rose. Il méditait deux fois par jour, souvent pour nettoyer son esprit d'idées reçues en matière de design. Il aimait aborder chaque nouvelle journée avec un esprit libre, ouvert et créatif. Au plafond, avec du bois et de la fibre de verre, il a créé la silhouette d'un étudiant zen s'agenouillant devant son maître.

Links: Das Ziel von James Rose war die völlige Verschmelzung von natürlicher Landschaft und vom Menschen gestalteter Welt. Die Zimmer wurden so angelegt, dass man die Natur direkt sehen und erfahren konnte. Rose entwarf alles im Haus selbst, auch das organische Sofa und den Tisch aus Alteisen und Holzresten.
Rechte Seite: Harmonie, Stille und Einfachheit waren grundlegend für das Credo von James Rose. Er meditierte zweimal täglich in seinem Zendo mit der Absicht, seinen Kopf freizumachen von vorgefassten Designideen, denn er wollte jeden Tag frei, unbefangen und kreativ angehen. An der Decke gestaltete Rose aus Holz und Glasfaser die Silhouette eines Zen-Schülers, der sich vor seinem Meister verneigt.

Previous pages: The James Rose residence and woodland along the Delaware River are now a noted study center for architecture and landscape design. The structure seems to have sprouted among the birches and elm trees. A bridge links the two segments of the roof garden. A wall of fibreglass, part of it set on the diagonal, is a screen for changing shadows of leaves and branches. Murals and shoji screens help blur the indoor/outdoor surfaces.
Right: At the entrance to the Zendo is a Rose-designed table.

Doubles pages précédentes: La maison et le domaine boisé de James Rose, sur la rive du Delaware, sont devenus un important centre de recherche en architecture et paysagisme. La structure semble avoir surgi d'elle-même entre les bouleaux et les ormes. Une passerelle relie deux tronçons du toit aménagé en jardin suspendu. Un mur en fibre de verre dont un pan est oblique sert d'écran où se projettent les ombres changeantes du feuillage et des branchages. Des peintures murales et des cloisons japonaises contribuent à faire disparaître les limites entre l'intérieur et l'extérieur.
A droite: à l'entrée du «zendo», une table dessinée par Rose.

Vorhergehende Doppelseiten: Das Wohngebäude und Waldstück von James Rose am Delaware River sind heute ein bekanntes Studienzentrum für Architektur und Landschaftsdesign. Das Gebäude wirkt wie natürlich zwischen den Birken und Ulmen emporgewachsen. Eine Brücke verbindet die beiden Bereiche der Dachterrasse. Eine zum Teil diagonal versetzt eingebaute Glasfaserwand bildet den Hintergrund für das lebhafte Schattenspiel von Zweigen und Blättern. Wandmalereien und japanische Shoji-Schiebetüren heben den Unterschied zwischen innen und außen auf.
Rechts: Am Eingang zum Zendo, dem Meditationsraum, steht ein von Rose entworfener Tisch.

Facing page: Rose designed the iron serpent fountain, visible from all rooms.
Above: A summer bedroom overlooking a mediation garden also serves as a small lecture room.
Right: In the dining room, a shoji screen panel moves back and forth to adjust light and shade, and to provide privacy. The mural on the right, called "The River of Hospitality", was crafted of concrete inset with dark pebbles, and runs continuously through to an exterior wall.

Page de gauche: Rose a dessiné la fontaine métallique en forme de serpent, visible depuis toutes les pièces.
Ci-dessus: Cette chambre à coucher d'été donnant sur un jardin de méditation sert également de petite salle de conférence.
A droite: Dans la salle à manger, une cloison «shoji» coulisse pour régler l'intensité de la lumière et fournir un peu d'intimité. La mosaïque sur la droite, intitulée «La rivière de l'hospitalité», est en ciment incrusté de galets sombres et se poursuit jusque sur un mur à l'extérieur.

Linke Seite: Rose entwarf den Brunnen mit der eisernen Schlange, der von allen Räumen aus sichtbar ist.
Oben: Dieses Sommerschlafzimmer mit Blick in den Meditationsgarten dient auch als kleiner Vortragsraum.
Rechts: Im Esszimmer kann die Shoji-Tür vor- und zurückgeschoben werden, um die Lichtverhältnisse zu ändern oder die Privatsphäre zu schützen. Das Mosaik an der Wand rechts, »River of Hospitality«, besteht aus Beton, in den dunkle Kieselsteine eingelassen sind. Es verläuft durch die Wand und ist auch auf der Außenseite zu sehen.

John Solomon

Glendale, Southern California

Dans la culture populaire, la Californie du sud est perçue comme une mosaïque onirique, où le bleu des piscines se mêle au vert des feuilles de palmiers, où les entrelacs des échangeurs d'autoroutes grouillent de décapotables. Juste à la lisière des lueurs clinquantes de Los Angeles s'étendent les vestiges vert pâle d'un désert primordial aux collines ondoyantes couleur de sauge, aux chênes séculaires et aux épinaies broussailleuses. Pendant les étés cuisants, l'air brûlant semble vibrer du grésillement des feuilles qui se racornissent et des hurlements inquiétants des coyotes. En 1964, Richard Neutra a construit cette maison dans un coin reculé de Glendale. Sa structure épurée tout en lignes horizontales et verticales illustre parfaitement la thèse du célèbre architecte: «Il faut placer l'homme en relation avec la nature; c'est là qu'il s'épanouit et qu'il se sent le plus chez lui.» Né à Vienne en 1892, Neutra s'est établi à Los Angeles en 1925. Avec sa femme Dione, il a créé des maisons modernes qui associaient une ossature métallique légère, des panneaux de verre et des finitions en stuc, le tout leur conférant un aspect transparent et naturel.

Southern California, in the popular imagination, is a mosaic of dreamy blue swimming pools, green palm fronds, tangles of freeways, and bumper-to-bumper convertibles. Just beyond the flashy edges of Los Angeles lie soft green traces of the primordial desert with undulating sage-green hills, archetypal ancient oaks, and scrubby chapparal. In super-heated summers, the charged air seems to vibrate with the sounds of crackling leaves and the eerie howl of coyotes. In a hidden corner of Glendale, architect Richard Neutra built this house in 1964. Its simple lines and post-and-beam construction perfectly illustrate his thesis: "Place man in relationship with nature; that's where he developed and where he feels most at home." Born in Vienna in 1892, Neutra established his practice in Los Angeles in 1925. With his wife, Dione, he created modernist houses which combined a light metal frame, panels of glass, and stucco finishes to finesse effortless appearance.

Bei Südkalifornien denkt jeder sofort an ein Mosaik von traumhaft schönen, blauen Pools und grünen Palmwedeln sowie an Cabrios, die Stoßstange an Stoßstange über ein Gewirr von Schnellstraßen rollen. Doch gleich außerhalb von Los Angeles finden sich zartgrüne Spuren einer urzeitlichen Wüste, mit grau-grün wogenden Hügeln, uralten Eichen und niedrigem »chapparal«-Gestrüpp. An extrem heißen Sommertagen scheint die Luft zu vibrieren, während man das Geräusch von knisterndem Laub und das unheimliche Heulen der Kojoten hört. In einer versteckten Ecke von Glendale baute der Architekt Richard Neutra 1964 dieses Haus. Die schlichte Linienführung und die Balken- und Pfahlkonstruktion illustrieren überzeugend seine These über Architektur: »Man muss den Menschen in Beziehung zur Natur setzen, denn er entstammt der Natur und hier fühlt er sich am wohlsten.« Neutra wurde 1892 in Wien geboren und eröffnete 1925 in Los Angeles sein Büro. Zusammen mit seiner Frau Dione schuf er modernistische Häuser, für die sie Metallrahmen, große Glasflächen und Mörtelputz kombinierten, was ihnen ein transparentes und scheinbar schwereloses Äußeres verleiht.

Previous pages: This house is the retreat of John Solomon, vice-president, Walt Disney Imagineering, who is responsible for creative development of Disney theme park attractions worldwide. In an alcove stands a pedestal jewelry table, an early design by George Nelson. The canvas is by Carl Ostendarp. Behind John Solomon a Claes Oldenburg "Plug" sculpture.
Above and right: "The house is sited beautifully to catch the sun and to make the most of the canyon views," noted John Solomon. "Neutra was a master at siting a house."

Double page précédente: Cette maison est le refuge de John Solomon, vice-président de Walt Disney Imagineering, responsable du développement des parcs d'attraction Disney dans le monde entier. Dans un coin, un coffret à bijoux monté sur pied, sous une toile signée George Nelson. Derrière John Solomon, une sculpture «prise de courant» de Claes Oldenburg.
Ci-dessus et à droite: «Neutra était maître en l'art de choisir l'emplacement d'une maison. Celle-ci est magnifiquement orientée de sorte à capter le soleil et à profiter au mieux de la vue sur le canyon», confie John Solomon.

Vorhergehende Doppelseite: Dieses Haus gehört John Solomon, Vizepräsident von Walt Disney Imagineering. Er ist verantwortlich für die Entwicklung der Disney-Themenparks in der ganzen Welt. In einer Nische steht ein Schmucktischchen, ein früher Entwurf von George Nelson. Das Gemälde ist von Carl Ostendarp. Hinter John Solomon hängt eine »Plug«-Skulptur von Claes Oldenburg.
Oben und rechts: »Das Haus liegt ideal, es fängt die Sonne und das Licht ein und man hat einen schönen Blick in den Canyon«, meint John Solomon. »Neutra verstand es meisterhaft, den richtigen Platz auszuwählen.«

Glendale, Southern California   John Solomon

Right: In the library, Solomon's collections include a classic Charles and Ray Eames rosewood-faced Lounge Chair, the design inspired by plywood splints. The screen of bent plywood is also by Charles and Ray Eames.
Below: In the living room, Solomon grouped a George Nelson "Coconut" chair from the 1950s, and a 1948 prototype of a three-legged coffee table by Charles and Ray Eames. The painting above the fireplace is by Richard Artschwager.

A droite: Dans la bibliothèque, les collections de Solomon incluent un classique du design : un fauteuil Lounge Chair avec un placage de bois de rose de Charles et Ray Eames. Le design est inspiré de civières en contre-plaqué.
Ci-dessous: Dans le salon, Solomon a assemblé un fauteuil «Coconut» de George Nelson, des années 1950, avec le prototype d'une table basse à trois pieds de Charles et Ray Eames datant de 1948. La peinture près de la cheminée est de Richard Artschwager.

Rechts: In der Bibliothek stehen Klassiker wie der Lounge Chair mit Palisanderfurnier von Charles und Ray Eames, das Design inspiriert sich an Schienen aus Sperrholz. Der Wandschirm aus gebogenem Schichtholz ist ebenfalls ein Entwurf von Charles und Ray Eames.
Unten: Im Wohnzimmer kombinierte Solomon einen »Coconut«-Stuhl von George Nelson aus den 1950ern mit dem Prototyp eines dreibeinigen Kaffeetisches von Charles und Ray Eames von 1948. Das Gemälde neben dem Kamin ist von Richard Artschwager.

Facing page: A sliding glass door opens the tile-walled bathroom to a partially enclosed garden courtyard.
Above: What year is it? In a corner of the time-warp Neutra-designed kitchen, Solomon gathered an original pair of Eames chairs and an Isamu Noguchi table. Solomon has been collecting mid-century modern furniture for more than 20 years.
Right: Beside the bed is an Ericofon telephone from the 1950s. The vase on the table is a Royal Copenhagen design by Nils Thorsson.

Page de gauche: Dans la salle de bains aux murs carrelés, une porte en verre coulissante s'ouvre sur une cour-jardin partiellement close.
Ci-dessus: En quelle année sommes-nous? Dans un coin de la cuisine conçue par Neutra pour déjouer le temps, Solomon a réuni une paire d'authentiques chaises de Charles et Ray Eames et une table d'Isamu Noguchi. Solomon collectionne les meubles modernes du milieu du 20ᵉ siècle depuis plus de vingt ans.
A droite: près du lit, un téléphone Ericofon des années 1950. Le vase sur le guéridon est une création de Nils Thorsson pour la manufacture Royal Copenhagen.

Linke Seite: Eine Glasschiebetür führt von dem gefliesten Badezimmer zu einem teilweise ummauerten Innenhof.
Oben: In welchem Jahr befinden wir uns? Die von Richard Neutra entworfene Küche nimmt mit auf eine Zeitreise; in einer Ecke stehen ein Originalstuhlpaar von Eames und ein Tisch von Isamu Noguchi. Solomon sammelt seit mehr als 20 Jahren Möbel aus den 1950ern.
Rechts: Neben dem Bett steht ein Ericofon-Telefon aus den 1950er Jahren. Die Vase auf dem Tisch in ein Entwurf von Nils Thorsson für die Porzellanmanufaktur Royal Copenhagen.

Ted Wells

Laguna Niguel, Southern California

Tous les samedi matin, l'architecte Ted Wells saute de son lit, se presse un verre de jus d'orange frais et médite sur le même petit problème : où son imagination débordante va-t-elle l'entraîner aujourd'hui? Ted, qui est également décorateur et paysagiste, vit au beau milieu du paradis des surfeurs et des adeptes du vélo tout-terrain. Laguna Niguel, à mi-chemin entre Los Angeles et San Diego, est une enclave écologique férocement protégée, le parc national de Cleveland Forest, qui compte également des kilomètres de plages de rêve. Ted va-t-il prendre sa planche de surf sous le bras et descendre à Salt Creek Beach, une plage abritée où les vagues rivalisent de beauté? Ou enfilera-t-il sa tenue de cycliste pour pédaler jusqu'au canyon d'Aliso Woods et tester ses muscles et son endurance sur les pentes abruptes? Cette fois, c'est la mer qui l'emporte. Le soir venu, l'infatigable Wells retrouve sa maison entourée de pins pierreux et de vieux eucalyptus qui soupirent et bruissent dans la brise. Il s'est créé ici un antre sur mesure qui inspire le repos de l'âme.

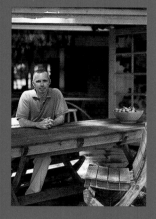

When architect Ted Wells leaps out of bed on sunny Saturday mornings, he squeezes a quick glass of fresh orange juice and ponders his one small problem: where will his restless imagination take him today? Ted, who also designs interiors and landscapes, lives in the middle of a surfer's and mountain biker's paradise. Laguna Niguel, midway between Los Angeles and San Diego, is a dreamy enclave of fiercely protected open spaces, the Cleveland National Forest, and miles of beautiful beaches. Should he grab his surfboard and drive to Salt Creek Beach, a sheltered cove with consistently beautiful waves? Or should he pull on his cycling gear and pedal out to Aliso Woods Canyon and challenge his strength and stamina on the steep curves? The beach calls. When the lively Wells returns home, he is surrounded by stone pines and old eucalyptus trees which sigh and shimmy in the wind. Here he has crafted a fine-tuned house that inspires spiritual repose.

Wenn sich der Architekt Ted Wells an einem sonnigen Samstagmorgen aus dem Bett schwingt, hat er, nachdem er seinen frischgepressten Orangensaft getrunken hat, eigentlich nur ein Problem: Was soll er mit dem Tag anfangen? Ted, der auch Innen- und Landschaftsarchitekt ist, lebt in einem Paradies für Surfer und Mountainbiker: Laguna Niguel, auf halbem Weg zwischen Los Angeles und San Diego, ist eine verträumte Enklave aus streng geschützter offener Landschaft, dem Cleveland National Forest und wunderbaren kilometerlangen Stränden. Soll er heute sein Surfbrett nehmen und zum Salt Creek Beach fahren, einer geschützten kleinen Bucht mit garantiert wunderbaren Wellen? Oder soll er sich lieber in seine Fahrradmontur werfen und zum Aliso Woods Canyon radeln – dann könnte er seine Kraft und Ausdauer an den Haarnadelkurven testen? Heute ruft der Strand. Wenn Wells dann nach Hause kommt, erwarten ihn Pinien und alte Eukalyptusbäume, die sich im Wind wiegen und seufzen. Hier hat er für sich selbst ein ganz besonderes Haus geschaffen, in dem der Geist zur Ruhe kommt.

First pages: *The house, with its shingled roof and stucco exterior, almost disappears among dry-stacked stone walls and the ghostly trunks of eucalyptus trees. Wells keeps his surfboard at the ready in his bedroom, for mornings when radio surf reports send a "surf's up" wave rave.*

Previous pages and below: *The dining room has new French doors which open directly to the shaded terrace. Wells keeps his connection with the garden constantly in view, even hanging branches of eucalyptus over the ceiling light above the dining table. Summer days here can be intensely hot, so Wells likes the stripped-down cool clarity of his rooms and prefers gleaming bare floors.*

Premières pages: *La maison, avec son toit en bardeaux et sa façade en stuc, disparaît presque parmi les murets en pierres sèches et les troncs fantomatiques des eucalyptus. Wells garde sa planche de surf toujours prête dans sa chambre, au cas où la radio du matin annoncerait que les vagues sont bonnes.*

Double page précédente et ci-dessous: *Les baies vitrées de la salle à manger s'ouvrent directement sur la terrasse. Wells ne perd jamais son jardin de vue, allant jusqu'à suspendre des branches d'eucalyptus au plafonnier au-dessus de la table de sa salle à manger. Ici, les journées d'été peuvent être torrides et il tient à ce que ses intérieurs restent dépouillés, clairs et frais, optant pour des sols nus et brillants.*

Eingangsseiten: *Mit seinem Schindeldach und gipsverputzten Außenwänden verschwindet das Haus fast zwischen den Trockenmauern und den gespenstischen Stämmen der Eukalyptusbäume. Das Surfbrett steht immer griffbereit im Schlafzimmer, für den Fall, dass morgens im Radio das heiß ersehnte »surf's up« gemeldet wird.*

Vorhergehende Doppelseite und unten: *Die deckenhohen neuen Verandatüren im Esszimmer führen direkt auf die schattige Terrasse und betonen die enge Verbindung zum Garten. Die Sommertage können hier sehr heiß werden, deshalb schätzt Ted Wells die zurückhaltende kühle Frische der Räume und der glänzenden nackten Fußböden.*

Wells' house, a spacious 1,900 square feet, was built in the sprawling
"ranch" style in the 1970s. Surprisingly, when Wells acquired it ten
years ago, the rooms were small, dark and poky, and decorated with
shag carpeting and elaborate flocked wallpaper. Wells opened up the
interiors, and simplified the architecture. New oak floors are now left
bare, and Wells has introduced the house to classic design decades
with Bertoia wire chairs, Le Corbusier leather chairs, and Eames's
classic plywood chairs.

Avec ses 180 mètres carrés, la spacieuse maison de Wells a été bâtie de
plein pied selon le plan du «ranch» des années 1970. Lorsque Wells l'a
achetée il y a dix ans, les pièces étaient exiguës et sombres, décorées
avec de la moquette à poils longs et des papiers peints floqués aux motifs chargés. Il a abattu des murs et simplifié l'architecture intérieure.
Les nouveaux parquets en chêne sont laissés nus et les pièces ont été
meublées avec des classiques du design tels que des fauteuils métal-
liques de Bertoia, des sièges en cuir de Le Corbusier et les fameuses
chaises en contre-plaqué d'Eames.

Wells geräumiges, gut 180 Quadratmeter großes Haus wurde in dem
für die 1970er Jahre typischen, großzügigen Ranch-Stil erbaut. Über-
raschenderweise waren die Räume klein, dunkel und verwinkelt, als
Wells das Haus vor zehn Jahren kaufte. Zottelige Teppiche und auf-
wändige Velourstapeten gehörten damals zur Ausstattung. Wells legte
einige Räume zusammen, um das Innere großzügiger zu gestalten
und die architektonische Struktur zu vereinfachen. Die neuen blanken
Eichenholzfußböden bieten jetzt den idealen Hintergrund für Design-
klassiker wie die Bertoia-Stühle aus Drahtgeflecht, die Lederstühle
von Le Corbusier und die berühmten Schichtholzstühle der Eames.

Silver Bullet Homes

Bisbee, Arizona

Les propriétaires collectionnent depuis longtemps avec passion les objets rétros américains. Ils commencèrent par les jouets avant de passer rapidement à la taille supérieure avec des juke-box des années 1940, des flippers des années 1950 puis des enseignes géantes au Néon. Leurs amis ne furent donc pas surpris quand ils s'intéressèrent aux vieilles caravanes. Ils rééquipèrent d'abord un «trailer» fait maison datant de 1952, puis un «Spartanette Tandem» de 1950, suivi d'un pompeusement nommé «Spartan Royal Mansion». En quête d'un lieu où conserver leurs trophées restaurés, ils achetèrent Shady Dell, un parc de caravanes fondé dans les années 1920 et aujourd'hui le plus vieux encore en activité en Arizona. Shady Dell possède également son restaurant sur roues, un «Valentine» des années 1950, qui se trouvait à l'origine à Wichita, dans le Kansas. Irrépressibles chineurs, les propriétaires ont récemment déniché un bus à soufflets de 1947, qu'ils ont converti en appartements privés, et un cabin-cruiser Chris-Craft de 1947, pour naviguer en toute sécurité sur la terre ferme.

The owners of these vintage trailers have long been avid collectors of Americana. "We love to collect American cultural icons," they stated. Starting with toys, they quickly moved on to grander objects – 1940s juke boxes, 1950s pinball machines and then large old neon signs. Perhaps vintage trailers came as no surprise to their friends, as they gathered and retrofitted first a homemade trailer from 1952, then a "Spartanette Tandem" from 1950, and the grandly named "Spartan Royal Mansion", 1951. In search of a place to park their restored trophies, the couple acquired the Shady Dell trailer park, founded in the 1920s and now the oldest continually operating trailer park in Arizona. Shady Dell is also equipped with a 1950s "Valentine" diner trailer originally operating in Wichita, Kansas. Irrepressible hunters, they recently found a 1947 flexible bus, which they have converted into living quarters, and a 1947 Chris-Craft cabin cruiser, for smooth sailing on dry land.

Die Besitzer sammeln schon seit langem begeistert alte Americana. »Wir lieben die kulturellen Ikonen Amerikas«, schwärmen sie. Zunächst begannen sie mit Spielzeug, bald jedoch gingen sie zu größeren Gegenständen über: Jukeboxes aus den 40ern, Fifties-Flipperautomaten und schließlich große alte Neonschilder. Für ihre Freunde war es deshalb auch keine Überraschung, als sie ihren ersten alten Wohnwagen kauften und umbauten, der 1952 in Eigenfertigung gebaut worden war. Danach kamen ein »Spartanette Tandem« von 1950 und ein Anhänger mit dem pompösen Namen »Spartan Royal Mansion« von 1951. Auf der Suche nach einem Platz für ihre restaurierten Trophäen kaufte das Paar den in den 1920er Jahren gegründeten Shady Dell Wohnwagenpark, der heute der älteste, ständig in Betrieb befindliche Wohnwagen-Park in Arizona ist. Hier findet sich auch ein »Valentine«-Diner aus den 1950ern, der ursprünglich in Wichita, Kansas, stand. Die Eigentümer suchen unermüdlich nach neuen Fundstücken und kauften vor kurzem einen Gelenkbus von 1947, den sie zu einer Kleinstwohnung umgestalteten, sowie einen Chris-Craft-Kajütkreuzer, ebenfalls von 1947, zum gemütlichen Segeln an Land.

Previous pages: The Shady Dell historic trailer camp in the summer sunshine in Bisbee, Arizona. The cozy 1950s trailer is neatly fitted with a plywood interior, a yellow and red "dinette", and vintage radios playing 1940s music. Trailers from the 1950s in superb condition like this one are very desirable for American vintage trailers collectors.
Right and below: The Shady Dell trailers are for rent for as little as $35 a night, but the couple prefers true trailer aficionados who stay a week or a month in their "El Rey", "Crown", "Silver Bullet" or "Airstream" trailers and time-travel back to idyllic 1950s America.

Doubles pages précédentes: le parc de caravanes anciennes Shady Dell. Ce trailer des années 1950 est aménagé avec des cloisons en contre-plaqué, un coin repas jaune et rouge et des radios anciennes qui passent de la musique des années 1940. Les caravanes des années 1950 en parfait état sont très recherchées par les collectionneurs.
A droite et ci-dessous: Ce couple de New-yorkais passera sa lune de miel dans le trailer «Airstream», aux dômes avant et arrière en aluminium poli. Les trailers de Shady Dell se louent à partir de 35 dollars la nuit, mais ici on préfère les aficionados qui restent une semaine ou un mois dans leur «El Rey», leur «Crown», leur «Silver Bullet» ou leur «Airstream» et remontent le temps pour se replonger dans l'Amérique des années 1950.

Vorhergehende Doppelseiten: der historische Shady Dell Wohnwagen-Park in Bisbee, Arizona, im Sonnenschein. Das gemütliche Wohnmobil aus den 1950ern ist innen mit Sperrholz verkleidet und verfügt über eine gelb-rote Essecke und ein altes Radio, das Original-Musik aus den 40ern spielt. Fifties-Wohnmobile in hervorragendem Zustand wie dieses sind bei Sammlern sehr beliebt.
Rechts und unten: Die Wohnmobile in Shady Dell kosten pro Nacht nur 35 Dollar, aber das Paar vermietet seine Wohnwagen am liebsten an echte Wohnwagenfans, die eine Woche oder sogar einen Monat in ihrem »El Rey«, »Crown«, »Silver Bullet« oder »Airstream« bleiben und sich auf eine Zeitreise in die idyllischen American Fifties begeben.

Above and right: *The streamlined "Spartan Royal Mansion", 1951, has polished birch plywood interiors, and is equipped with a ceiling air cooler, a monitor which plays vintage films and television programs, and a working vintage stove.*
Following pages: *A New York couple married in vintage style in Bisbee, then spent their honeymoon in the "Airstream" trailer, complete with front and back ceiling domes made of reflective polished aluminum. The "Spartanette Tandem" trailer is popular for its authentic period style, down to the kitschy hand-printed fabrics, stove, wagon salt and pepper shakers, and neat-as-a-pin kitchenette.*

Ci-dessus et à droite: *L'intérieur de l'élégant «Spartan Royal Mansion», datant de 1951, est tapissé de placages en bouleau poli. Il est équipé d'un cooler de plafond, d'un écran qui passe des films et des programmes de télévision d'autrefois, et d'une cuisinière d'époque.*
Double page suivante: *Le trailer «Spartanette Tandem» est très apprécié pour son style authentique et kitsch, avec ses tissus imprimés à la main, sa cuisinière, sa salière et poivrière en forme de wagon et sa kitchenette immaculée.*

Oben und rechts: *Der stromlinienförmige »Spartan Royal Mansion« von 1951 ist innen mit glänzendem Birkensperrholz ausgekleidet. Zur Ausstattung gehören eine Klimaanlage, ein Fernseher, in dem alte Filme und Fernsehprogramme laufen, und ein alter Herd.*
Folgende Doppelseite: *Ein New Yorker Paar heiratete in Bisbee im Stil von früher und verbrachte seine Flitterwochen im »Airstream«-Wohnmobil, dessen kuppelförmige Vorder- und Rückfront aus reflektierendem, glänzendem Aluminium besteht. Der »Spartanette Tandem«-Wohnwagen ist bekannt für seinen authentischen zeitgetreuen Stil, bis hin zu kitschigen handbedruckten Stoffen, Herd, Salz- und Pfefferstreuern und einer winzigen Kochnische.*

Alex Willcock

Northern Victoria

«Vente du dernier recours». Cet appel désespéré dans un journal local attira l'attention d'Alex Willcock et l'amena à acquérir 26 hectares de terrain vierge dans le nord de l'Etat de Victoria. «Il n'y avait qu'une remise à tracteur sur les terres, qui se trouvent au milieu d'un parc boisé national, à des kilomètres de nulle part», se souvient Willcock. Directeur d'une agence londonienne de gestion de marques, il se rend sur sa propriété le plus souvent possible avec ses deux enfants, Coco et Felix, et sa compagne Charlie. «On a construit une maison en terre battue, avec des murs de 40 cm d'épaisseur érigés avec la terre du domaine. Ce sont de parfaits isolants naturels» explique Willcock. Là, ils vivent dans un monde écologiquement parfait. L'eau de pluie est collectée dans de grandes citernes en béton. L'éclairage et la pompe à eau fonctionnent à l'énergie solaire. «Le vaste espace de séjour est incroyablement adaptable» observe Willcock. «On peut rassembler les chaises et le canapé autour du feu, ou les repousser contre les murs quand on donne une fête. C'est un endroit idéal pour se détendre».

"Desperation sale." The dramatic plea in a country newspaper caught Alex Willcock's eye, and led him to acquire 51 acres of pristine land in Northern Victoria. "There was basically just a tractor shed on the land, which is in the middle of a national forest, and miles from anywhere," recalled Willcock. Director of a London branding agency, he visits the property as often as possible with his two children, Coco and Felix, and his partner, Charlie. "We built a rammed-earth house, with walls 16 inches thick, using soil from the property," Willcock said. "The earth walls are great natural insulators." His is an ecologically perfect world, with rainwater collected in large concrete water tanks. Solar power runs the water pump and lighting. "The large living space is incredibly adaptable," Willcock noted. "We can gather the chairs and sofa around the fire, or push them all back when we have a party. It's a great place in which to unwind your mind."

»Notverkauf«. Dieser Hilferuf in einer regionalen Tageszeitung stach Alex Willcock ins Auge und war Anlass für den Kauf von 20 Hektar unerschlossenem Land im Norden des australischen Bundesstaates Victoria. »Eigentlich gab es dort nur einen Traktorschuppen«, erinnert sich Willcock. »Das Land liegt in einem Naturschutzgebiet, meilenweit von jeglicher Zivilisation entfernt.« Der Direktor einer Londoner Branding-Agentur fährt so oft wie möglich mit seinen beiden Kindern Coco und Felix und seiner Partnerin Charlie dorthin. »Wir bauten ein Haus aus gestampfter Erde und Lehm, mit 40 Zentimeter dicken Wänden. Dabei verwendeten wir Erde von dem Grundstück«, erzählt Willcock. »Die Erdwände isolieren fantastisch gegen die Hitze.« Sein Haus ist so weit wie möglich ökologisch ausgerichtet: Er sammelt das Regenwasser in großen Betontanks, während die Wasserpumpe und das elektrische Licht mit Solarenergie betrieben werden. »Das große Wohnzimmer ist unglaublich anpassungsfähig«, sagt Willcock. »Wir können die Stühle und das Sofa um den Kamin herum gruppieren oder alles an die Wand stellen, wenn wir eine Party geben. Ein herrlicher Ort zum Entspannen.«

Alex Willcock's Australian country house stands on a hilltop overlooking natural lakes, eucalyptus forests, and 40 miles of wild nature in all directions. "You sometimes wonder if there is another world," said Willcock. "It's magical." It's built of rammed earth with a corrugated steel roof. Many of the architectural materials in the house – the doors and the windows, for example – were salvaged and recycled. From the terrace he and his children watch kangaroos grazing. In the evenings native cockatoos and pink and red rosellas roost and squawk in the scrubby eucalyptus trees.

La maison de campagne australienne d'Alex Willcock se dresse au sommet d'une colline qui domine des lacs naturels, des forêts d'eucalyptus et une soixantaine de kilomètres de nature sauvage qui s'étire dans toutes les directions. «On se demande parfois si on n'est pas dans un autre monde. C'est magique», confie Willcock. La maison est construite en terre battue avec un toit en tôle d'acier ondulée. Une grande partie des matériaux de construction ont été récupérés ailleurs et recyclés. Depuis la terrasse, Alex et ses enfants observent les kangourous qui broutent. Le soir, les cacatoès et les grandes perruches roses et rouges viennent nicher et roucouler dans les branches des eucalyptus.

Alex Willcocks australisches Landhaus steht allein auf einem Hügel, mit Panoramablick auf Seen, Eukalyptuswälder und 60 Kilometer unberührte Natur in jede Richtung. »Manchmal fragt man sich, ob es noch eine andere Welt gibt«, meint Willcock. »Es ist wirklich herrlich hier.« Das Haus ist aus gestampfter Erde und Lehm gebaut und hat ein Dach aus Wellblech. Viele der hier verwendeten Baumaterialien stammen aus abgerissenen Häusern, so auch die Türen und Fenster. Von der Terrasse aus beobachten Alex und die Kinder Kängurus. Abends versammeln sich Kakadus sowie pinkfarbene und rote Sittiche unter lautem Gekreische in den Eukalyptusbäumen.

Previous pages: *The large fireplace circulates hot air through the house. The red and white quilt, designed by Alex Willcock and David Band, was made in Ahmedabad, India.*
Above: *The main bedroom in the farmhouse was designed for utmost simplicity and to feel like an traditional country bedroom.*

Double page précédente: *La grande cheminée fait circuler de l'air chaud dans toute la maison. La tenture rouge et blanche, dessinée par Alex Willcock et David Band, a été confectionnée à Ahmedabad.*

Ci-dessus: *La chambre principale a été conçue dans un souci de simplicité absolue, comme une chambre rustique traditionnelle.*

Vorhergehende Doppelseite: *Der große Kamin heizt das ganze Haus. Der rot-weiße Quilt, den Alex Willcock und David Band entwarfen, wurde in Ahmedabad in Indien angefertigt.*
Oben: *Für das Hauptschlafzimmer in dem Farmhaus galt das Gebot größtmöglicher Schlichtheit, denn es sollte wie ein traditionelles Farmhausschlafzimmer aussehen.*

Northern Victoria

Alex Willcock

The wonderfully utilitarian bath was improvised with an industrial steel bath, formerly used for rinsing organic vegetables. "We keep everything basic at the house," Willcock said. "We want to spend time outdoors, riding horses, going on picnics, exploring the region, meeting old friends."

Cette magnifique baignoire improvisée était à l'origine une cuve industrielle en acier servant à laver des légumes issus de l'agriculture biologique. «Dans la maison, nous veillons à ce que tout reste rudimentaire», explique Willcock. «Nous voulons passer nos journées au dehors, à monter à cheval, faire des pique-niques, explorer la région, retrouver de vieux amis».

Für das herrlich praktische Badezimmer funktionierte man eine Stahlwanne, in der ursprünglich biologisch angebautes Gemüse gewaschen wurde, um zu einer Badewanne. »Wir wollten alles im Haus so einfach wie möglich halten«, erklärt Willcock. »Wir sind viel draußen, reiten, machen Picknicks und besuchen alte Freunde«.

Living in Bombala

Monaro Plains, New South Wales

Autrefois, les Australiens qualifiaient leur isolement géographique de «tyrannie de la distance». Aujourd'hui, ils considèrent comme une bénédiction d'être à l'écart du reste du monde. A mi-chemin entre Sydney et Melbourne se trouve la petite ville de Bombala, si discrète qu'il suffit d'un instant d'inattention sur la route pour la rater. La région est célèbre pour sa pêche à la truite et ses populations amicales d'ornithorynques qui se promènent le soir sur leurs fameux pieds palmés. C'est ici, dans les plaines isolées de Monaro, qu'un homme d'affaires a choisi de bâtir son refuge. Il a demandé au cabinet d'architecture Collins, Collins & Turner de lui en dresser les plans. Il habitait alors à New York tandis que Penny Collins et Huw Turner travaillaient à Londres et Ian Collins à Sydney. Après s'être rendus trois fois sur les lieux, les architectes ont utilisé des logiciels de design assisté par l'Internet pour échanger des photos numériques et des plans. Le client voulait que sa maison évoque un bâtiment de ferme, dépouillé et fonctionnel – seules les formes pures et abstraites restent dans la mémoire.

Australians once called their geographical remoteness, "the tyranny of distance". Today, they glory in living off the map, and consider it a blessing to be far from the rest of the world. Halfway between Sydney and Melbourne lies the blink-and-you'll-miss-it town of Bombala. The region is noted for its exceptional trout fishing, and for friendly populations of platypus, who promenade in the evening on their distinctive web feet. Here, a businessman chose to build a retreat on the remote Monaro Plains. He commissioned the architectural firm of Collins, Collins & Turner to plan his house. He was in New York. Penny Collins and Huw Turner were working in London, and Ian Collins was in Sydney. The design team made three visits to the site, and used CAD and the internet to exchange digital photography and emails. The client wanted a house reminiscent of a farm building, pared down and functional – only the pure forms to be remembered.

Früher sprachen die Australier von der »Tyrannei der Entfernung«. Heute sind sie froh und glücklich darüber, so weit weg vom Rest der Welt zu leben. Auf halbem Weg zwischen Sydney und Melbourne liegt Bombala, eine Kleinstadt und so winzig, dass man sie leicht verpasst, wenn man nicht schnell vom Gaspedal geht. Diese Gegend ist bekannt für ihre hervorragenden Forellen und die freundlichen Schnabeltiere, die abends auf großen Schwimmfüßen umherstrolchen. Hier, mitten in den einsam gelegenen Monaro Plains, beschloss ein Geschäftsmann sein Landhaus zu errichten und beauftragte das Londoner Architekturbüro Collins, Collins & Turner mit dem Entwurf. Er selbst lebt in New York. Penny Collins und Huw Turner arbeiteten in London und Ian Collins in Sydney. Dreimal war das Architektenteam vor Ort. Mit Hilfe von CAD und Internet tauschten sie Emails und digitale Fotos aus. Der Kunde wollte ein Haus, das an ein Farmgebäude erinnern sollte, einfach, zurückhaltend, schlicht und funktionell – nur reine abstrakte Formen.

The Bombala house, with a nod to Philip Johnson's New Canaan Glass House, revels in its elegant simplicity and formal geometry. Architects Collins, Collins & Turner used a rigorously edited palette of materials and restrained detailing to focus attention on the abstract forms. Selecting a standard steel frame and standard aluminum glazing sections, concrete and corrugated iron, the architects saved money for the double-height living room and luxurious fittings and fixtures.

La maison de Bombala, qui rend un discret hommage à la maison de verre de Philip Johnson à New Canaan, associe une élégante simplicité et une géométrie formelle. Collins, Collins & Turner ont utilisé une palette de matières triées sur le volet et ont limité les détails afin de centrer toute l'attention sur les formes abstraites. En choisissant une structure standard en acier et des encadrements de portes et de fenêtres en aluminium, béton et tôle ondulée, les architectes ont économisé de quoi créer la double hauteur sous plafond du salon et l'équiper luxueusement.

In seiner eleganten Schlichtheit und mit seinen formal-geometrischen Elementen ist das Bombala-Haus eine Hommage an Philip Johnsons »Glass House« in New Canaan, Connecticut. Die Architekten Collins, Collins & Turner verwendeten eine eng begrenzte Palette von Materialien und Details, um die abstrakten Formen zur Geltung zu bringen. Für die Fensterbereiche wählten sie Standardrahmen aus Stahl und Aluminium, sie arbeiteten mit Beton und Wellblech, um Geld für den luxuriösen Wohnbereich mit doppelter Raumhöhe zu sparen.

Notes / Notes / Hinweise

The Groddagården Museum in Northern Gotland is open from May to August:
Le musée Groddagården au nord de l'île de Gotland, est ouvert de mai à août:
Das Museum Groddagården im Norden von Gotland ist von Mai bis August geöffnet:
> Fleringe
> 62034 Lärbro
> Sweden
> T +46-498-224 535

The Russel Wright Design Center is open by appointment for guided tours:
Le Russel Wright Design Center se visite sur rendez-vous avec un conférencier:
Das Russel Wright Design Center ist nach Anmeldung für Führungen geöffnet:
> Manitoga
> P.O. Box 249, Route 9D
> Garrison, NY 10524
> USA
> T +1-845-424-3812
> F +1-845-424-4043
> info@russelwrightcenter.org
> www.russelwrightcenter.org

The James Rose Center for Landscape Architectural Research and Design is open by appointment:
Le centre de recherche en architecture et paysagisme James Rose se visite sur rendez-vous:
Das James Rose Center for Landscape Architectural Research and Design ist nach Anmeldung für Besucher geöffnet:
> 506 East Ridgewood Avenue
> Ridgewood, NJ 07450
> USA
> T +1-201-446-6017
> cardasis@larp.umass.edu
> www.jamesrosecenter.org